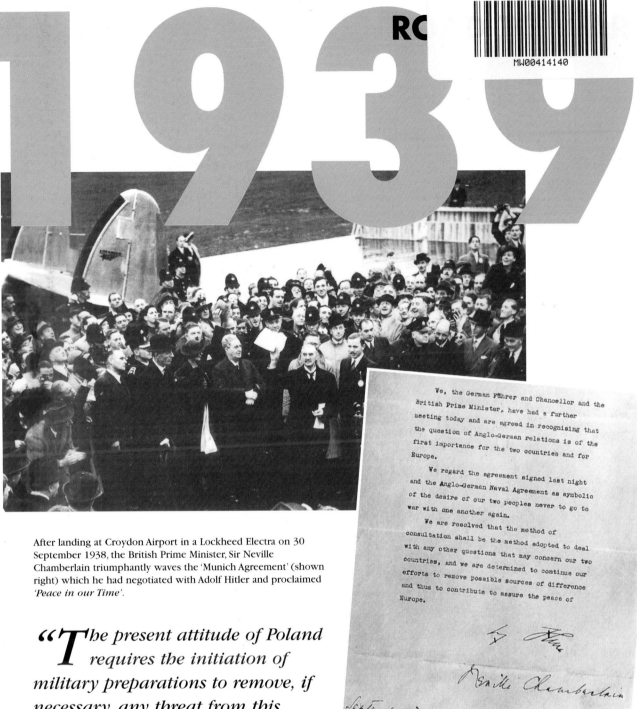

After landing at Croydon Airport in a Lockheed Electra on 30 September 1938, the British Prime Minister, Sir Neville Chamberlain triumphantly waves the 'Munich Agreement' (shown right) which he had negotiated with Adolf Hitler and proclaimed *'Peace in our Time'*.

We, the German Führer and Chancellor and the British Prime Minister, have had a further meeting today and are agreed in recognising that the question of Anglo-German relations is of the first importance for the two countries and for Europe.

We regard the agreement signed last night and the Anglo-German Naval Agreement as symbolic of the desire of our two peoples never to go to war with one another again.

We are resolved that the method of consultation shall be the method adopted to deal with any other questions that may concern our two countries, and we are determined to continue our efforts to remove possible sources of difference and thus to contribute to assure the peace of Europe.

September 30, 1938

"The present attitude of Poland requires the initiation of military preparations to remove, if necessary, any threat from this direction forever.

"The aim will be to destroy Polish military strength and create in the East a situation which satisfies the requirements of national defence. The Free State of Danzig will be proclaimed a part of Reich Territory at the outbreak of hostilities, at the latest.

"The political leaders consider it their task to isolate Poland if possible, that is to say to limit the war to Poland only. The development of increasing internal crises in France and the resulting British cautiousness may produce such a situation in the not too distant future."

'Contingency White', Hitler's directive to the German armed forces

3 April 1939

1938-1939

Left: On 29 September 1938, Sir Neville Chamberlain flew to München (Munich) and was met at the airport by Joachim von Ribbentrop, the German Foreign Minister, and other high ranking party officials. He is seen here being escorted to his meeting with Hitler in the 'Führerhaus' in the Königsplatz, München.

Above: The two dictators Adolf Hitler and Benito Mussolini prior to the signing of the 'Pact of Steel', which was formally signed in the Reich Chancellery, Berlin on 22 May 1939 amid considerable pomp and ceremony, binding Italy and Germany together in a military alliance.

Above: On 24 August, von Ribbentrop returned from signing the German Soviet Pact aboard the Fw 200 A-08 W.Nr. 3098 named *GRENZMARK* carrying the civil code D-ACVH. The negotiations had been carried out in the strictest secrecy and the Pact was formally signed on 23 August 1939.

Right: The Russian Foreign Minister, Vyacheslav Molotov (left) in discussion with Hitler, through an interpreter (centre), prior to the signing on the German Soviet Pact.

Road to War

When Hitler came to power in 1933, the German people were still smarting from the harsh restrictions placed on their country by the Treaty of Versailles. The new leader restored national pride, first by re-occupying the Rhineland, and then by the annexation of Austria into the German Reich. These actions drew little protest from Britain and France, but the proposed entry into the Sudetenland of Czechoslovakia with its large German minority, did cause an international crisis. In September 1938, the British Government, under Neville Chamberlain, agreed to allow Germany to march into the area, hoping that this would signal the end of Hitler's aspirations on European territory. This hope was dashed when German troops entered Bohemia and Moravia on 15 March 1939, having already isolated Slovakia. The invasion was supported by 500 Luftwaffe aircraft but, unlike in Austria, no senior commanders or nucleus of élite pilots was gained as a result - in fact large numbers of Czech pilots escaped to bolster the British and French Air Forces. Eight days later, Memel was annexed from the Baltic state of Lithuania and then Germany turned its sights to Poland.

Hitler had long resented the 'Polish Corridor' which separated Germany from East Prussia and contained Danzig, an old German city given an international status in 1919. At a lunch at the Grand Hotel in Berchtesgaden on 24 October 1939, Hitler's Foreign Minister, Joachim von Ribbentrop, suddenly proposed to the Polish Ambassador to Berlin, Józef Lipski, the restoration of Danzig to Germany and the building of a road and railway across the Polish corridor. Unlike the Czech Government, the Poles refused to be intimidated and, on 31 March 1939, the British Prime Minister, Neville Chamberlain, announced that his country would guarantee immediate military aid to Poland should its independence be threatened. This support was in addition to a Franco-Polish treaty which had been signed in 1921 and never revoked.

Britain also began a wary series of negotiations with Russia, but these never really got off the ground. The Soviet leader Stalin's main aim at this time was to buy time in order to counter a German attack which he knew would eventually materialise from the west. Paradoxically, therefore, in August 1939, Stalin drew up an agreement with Hitler which provided for the division of Poland between them, and effectively opened the way for Germany to invade. Previously, on 22 May 1939, Germany and Italy signed 'the pact of steel' and moves were made to bring Japan into a triple alliance. Thus the seeds were sown for war, with Britain, France and Poland on one side and Germany, Italy and Japan on the other. The USA remained deeply isolationist at this time, and was not drawn into the war until December 1941.

On 21 April 1938, a memorial parade was held at Berlin-Döberitz to commemorate the twentieth anniversary of the death of Manfred von Richthofen. Included in the personalities present were von Richthofen's mother, his younger brother, Göring and several officers from the new Jagdgeschwader 'Richthofen'. Among these were the Kommodore, Oberst Gerd von Massow (with helmet to the left of Göring who is holding up his Field Marshall's baton) and on either side of the flag on the left are two other pilots: Lt. Heino Greisert and Lt. Hermann Reifferscheidt. The flag is the banner of I./JG 131 'Richthofen', the other belongs to the second Gruppe. The Fokker Triplane in the centre of the photograph was similar to that in which von Richthofen was killed.

RIGHT : The Jagdwaffe grew at an extraordinary rate from 1936 and its units were continuously enlarged and redesignated. The I./JG 131 was established on 1 April 1937 at Jesau airfield in East Prussia, having been formed from pilots and ground personnel provided by JG 132 'Richthofen'. Here, the Gruppenkommandeur, Hptm. Bernhard Woldenga is shown sat in the cockpit of his Bf 109 D which was fitted with an ESK 2000a Schiesskamera (gun camera) above the port wing. The Gruppe's emblem, the 'Jesau Kreuz', is painted below the cockpit. This would continue to appear on the unit's Bf 109s for several years even after the unit was redesignated III./JG 27 (see also Section One, Birth of the Luftwaffe, page 80).

**The 'Jesau Kreuz' of I./JG 131
(later I./JG 1)**

ABOVE: This photograph of a Bf 109 E was taken at Vörden airfield late 1939 gives excellent detail of the Jesau Kreuz badge.

RIGHT: Three officers from I./JG 131 at Jesau pose in front of a Bf 109 D during the summer of 1938. From left are: Oblt. Erhard Braune, Lt. Erwin Mann and Oblt. Schneider. The white circle painted around the aircraft's spinner indicates that it belonged to the Gruppenstab.

RIGHT: A group of family and friends of the Gräfin (countess) Siersdorf relax at Oppeln just after the Munich crisis in the autumn of 1938. At this time several officers from 2./JG 131 were billeted in the countess' home. See also photo at top of page 81 in Section 1, Birth of the Luftwaffe. The partially hidden 'Jesau Kreuz' emblem of the first Gruppe of JG 131 can be seen on the Bf 109 D in the background, coded 'Red 5'.

Spinner colours of Bf 109 D, 'Red 3' of 2./JG 131. RLM 70 at the front with RLM 23 at the rear divided by a white circle in the centre.

ABOVE: A Bf 109 D, coded 'Red 3' of 2./JG 131, shown following a belly landing at Liegnitz during the autumn of 1938. Like 'Red 5' above, the uppersurfaces are painted black-green (RLM 70) with light blue (RLM 65) underneath.

LEFT AND ABOVE: Two views of a Bf 109 D of 1./JG 131 shown after being badly damaged at Jesau during the summer of 1938. At this time German fighter aircraft had black-green (RLM 70) and dark green (RLM 71) uppersurfaces with pale blue (RLM 65) beneath.

1938–1939

ABOVE: Throughout the late summer of 1938 the Luftwaffe was expanding at a rapid rate with many new units being formed. Here pilots and mechanics from I./JG 231 are assembled in front of their new Bf 109Ds. This unit was renamed I./ZG 2 for only a short time in 1939 before being renamed again JGr 102 on 21 September 1939. This unit carried the 'Bernburger Jäger' badge which had been carried over from when the unit was known as 1./JG 137 and I./ZG 2. The first Staffel also carried the emblem of a black hand on a white circle on the nose.

RIGHT: Lt. Gerhard Granz of 1./ZG 2 sits in the cockpit of his Bf 109 D 'White 11' in 1939, while mechanics top up the fuel tank and make final pre flight checks on the engine. Note the position of the fuel intake just below the cockpit.

Emblem of 1./JG 231 and I./ZG 2

ABOVE AND LEFT: Two views of what looks like an almost brand new Bf 109 D, coded 'Red 10' of 2./JG 131 which overturned and was severely damaged at Jesau during late summer 1938. The aircraft was finished in dark-green (RLM 70) uppersurfaces and pale-blue (RLM 65) underneath. The spinner appears to be white with a thin red band at the rear.

RIGHT: The second highest scoring ace in the Legion Condor, Hptm. Wolfgang Schellmann (left) gives instructions to the pilots of 1./JG 131 'Richthofen' prior to a training flight during the winter of 1938-1939.

ABOVE AND RIGHT: Lt. Erich Kircheis in the cockpit of one of the first Bf 109 Ds delivered to Stab I./JG 233 at Bad Aibling in February 1939. Kircheis joined I./JG 233 in 1938 and was soon chosen by the Geschwaderkommodore, Theo Osterkamp, to take the position of Adjutant in the Geschwaderstab (note the single chevron which indicated this position). He stayed on as Adjutant until the Battle of Britain when he was shot down and taken prisoner. In the background is one of the unit's last remaining He 51s.

LEFT: A group of pilots probably from 3./JG 233 photographed at Bad Aibling during the spring of 1939 with a Bf 109 D in the background. I./JG 233 was to be redesignated I./JG 51 in May 1939. Formed mainly from Austrian pilots, 3./JG 51 was commanded by Hptm. Erich Gerlitz (left). Third from the left in this photo is Lt. Richard Leppla who was later awarded the Ritterkreuz.

ABOVE: Bf 109 Ds of the first Gruppe of Jagdgeschwader 'Richthofen' at combat readiness on Berlin-Döberitz airfield in March 1939, during the Czechoslovakian crisis.

Messerschmitt Bf 109 D-1 of 1./JG 131 (1./JG 2) 'Richthofen'
Flown by Lt. Hermann Reifferscheidt, March 1939, just prior to the German entry into Bohemia and Moravia on 15 March 1939. The aircraft was painted overall black-green (RLM 70) and carried the special markings adopted by JG 131's Schwarmführern at this time. The machine also had a variation of the familiar 'Richthofen Geschwader' badge painted on both sides of the fuselage.

Plan view showing the white markings on the uppersurfaces of Lt. Hermann Reifferscheidt's Bf 109 D-1.

Variant of JG 131 (later JG 2) 'Richthofen' badge

ABOVE: Taken at Berlin-Döberitz during the Czechoslovakian crisis of March 1939, this photo shows Bf 109 D, 'White 3' piloted by Lt. Hermann Reifferscheidt of 1./JG 131 (later 1./JG 2) 'Richthofen'. His aircraft carried the markings of large white crosses on the upper wings and fuselage sides with white question marks above the horizontal tail surfaces which identified him as one of the Staffel Schwarmführern.

ABOVE: Another Schwarmführer's aircraft, this time an early Bf 109 E-1 'Yellow 9' of 3./JG 131 (3./JG 2) preparing for take off during the Czechoslovakian crisis of March 1939. This aircraft also carried white diagonal crosses but those on the wing appear to be narrower and positioned nearer the wing Balkenkreuz. Unfortunately it is impossible to ascertain whether the tail surfaces also carry the similar white markings to those on the Bf 109 D shown at the top of the page.

RIGHT: Having been one of the first fifty 'Fliegeroffizieren' in the Austrian Air Force, Oblt. Erwin Bacsila entered the Luftwaffe after the annexation of Austria into the German Reich. Early in 1939 he was for a short time with I./JG 131 (later I./JG 2) before being transferred to I./JG 333 (later II./ZG 1). His incredible career will often be related in the course of this series as he served with, amongst others, JG 52, JG 77, Sturmstaffel 1, JG 3 and JG 400. Note his personal emblem, the abbreviation of his wife's first name Dorothea, on his Bf 109 D. The JG 2 'Richthofen' badge shows clearly by the broken lines on the script 'R' that it was applied with a stencil.

1938–1939

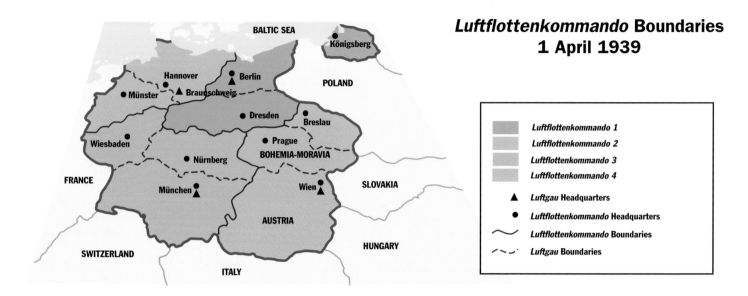

Luftflottenkommando Boundaries
1 April 1939

▨	*Luftflottenkommando 1*
▨	*Luftflottenkommando 2*
▨	*Luftflottenkommando 3*
▨	*Luftflottenkommando 4*
▲	*Luftgau* Headquarters
●	*Luftflottenkommando* Headquarters
⌒	*Luftflottenkommando* Boundaries
‑‑‑	*Luftgau* Boundaries

RIGHT: A Schwarm of Bf 109 Ds 'Red 4, 6 and 10' from 2./JG 131 (later 2./JG 2) photographed in March or April 1939 just before re-equipping with the Bf 109 E.

**JG 131 (later JG 2)
'Richthofen' badge**

ABOVE AND RIGHT: This Bf 109 D-1 'Red 11' of 2./JG 131 (later 2./JG 2) was photographed from both sides after making a wheels-up landing at Berlin-Döberitz airfield during the spring of 1939. Shortly after this, the unit was re-equipped with the Bf 109 E. Note the script 'R' badge of JG 2 painted on the fuselage sides with the 87 octane fuel filler position triangle painted below the cockpit in yellow outlined in white. At this time most Bf 109 Ds were painted in black-green (RLM 70) on the uppersurfaces with pale blue (RLM 65) underneath.

ABOVE: Ofw. Elster, Oberwerksmeister of 1./JG 2, relaxes in front of one of the unit's Bf 109 Ds during the spring of 1939. The aircraft carries number 'White 17'.

ABOVE: To the left of this photo is Hptm. Dr Erich Mix, Mayor of Wiesbaden, who flew as reserve officer in I./JG 334 (having been a fighter pilot during the First World War). He later became the Technical Officer of the Gruppe which was redesignated I./JG 53. The Leutnant in the centre has not been identified. To the right is Oblt. Rolf Pingel, Staffelkapitän of 2./JG 53.

LEFT: Following a training flight, two pilots in flying suits from 1./JG 2 discuss a maintenance problem with a mechanic, amongst other members of the unit sitting in front of one of the Staffel's Bf 109 Ds 'White 17' during the spring of 1939.

BELOW: Bf 109 Ds of I./JG 53 preparing for take-off from Wiesbaden–Erbenheim airfield in April 1939. These 'D' variants were soon to be replaced by 'Emils'.

ABOVE: Accidents were not uncommon with the Bf 109 E. Here 'White 5' of 1./JG 51 has flipped over on to its back at Bad Aibling following the collapse of its starboard undercarriage leg during a landing in the spring of 1939. Note the black-green (RLM 70) and light-blue (RLM 65) demarcation line running to the leading edge of the wing compared to the photo on the left.

LEFT: A group of Bf 109 Es of I./JG 233 (later I./JG 51) preparing for take off from Bad Aibling airfield around April 1939

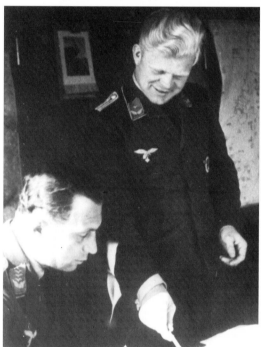

ABOVE: Facing the camera in uniform is Hptm. Hans-Heinrich Brustellin, Gruppenkommandeur of I./JG 233 (later I./JG 51), at Bad Aibling in April 1939. Brustellin was scheduled to take over J/88 from Hptm. Walter Grabmann but the war in Spain ended before this could take effect.

ABOVE: Hptm. Hans-Heinrich Brustellin, Gruppenkommandeur of I./JG 233 (seated) in conversation with Lt. Richard Leppla, of the third Staffel at Bad Aibling during April 1939. (Leppla was later awarded the Ritterkreuz).

RIGHT: On 3 November 1938, IV./JG 132 'Richthofen' was redesignated I./JG 331, becoming I./JG 77 in May 1939. This Bf 109 E, 'Red 12' (possibly W.Nr. 4065) probably photographed at Karlsbad early in 1939, retained the disc marking of the fourth Gruppe, but the famous script 'R' badge has not been applied. The aircraft was piloted by Lt. Helmut Lohoff who is sat in front of the cockpit. This aircraft also has yellow gun trays above the engine.

The Jagdwaffe

When the Spanish Civil War ended, the *Luftwaffe* had fifteen 'light' fighter units equipped in the main with the single–engined Bf 109, and eight 'heavy' fighter units intended to receive the Bf 110 twin-engined destroyer. Following the entry into Bohemia and Moravia in March 1939, yet another reorganisation took place in the *Luftwaffe's* area of command in order to bring the force to a more operational footing.

On 1 April the boundaries of the previous three *Luftwaffengruppenkommandos* were redrawn and increased to four, these being renamed *Luftflotten*. At the same time, a number of flexible operational commands with no fixed headquarters were established under the name *Fliegerdivision*. The new areas of command, their commanders and headquarters were (see Map 1 on page 202):

Gen.d.Fl. Albert Kesselring   Gen.d.FL. Hellmuth Felmy   Gen.d.Fl. Hugo Sperrle   Gen.d.Fl. Alexander Löhr

Luftflottenkommando 1	**Gen.d.Fl. Kesselring**	**Berlin**
Luftwaffenkommando Ostpreussen	Gen.Lt. Wimmer	Königsberg
Luftgau I	Gen.Maj. Mohr	Königsberg
Luftgau III	Gen.Maj. Weise	Berlin
Luftgau IV	Gen.Maj. Mayer	Dresden
1.Fliegerdivision	Gen.Lt. Grauert	
2.Fliegerdivision	Gen.Maj. Loerzer	
Luftflottenkommando 2	**Gen.d.Fl. Felmy**	**Braunschweig**
Luftgau VI	Gen.Maj. Schmidt	Münster
Luftgau XI	Gen.Maj. Wolf	Hannover
3.Fliegerdivision	Gen.Maj. Putzier	
4.Fliegerdivision	Gen.d.Fl. Keller	
7.Fliegerdivision	Gen.Maj. Student	
Luftflottenkommando 3	**Gen.d.Fl. Sperrle**	**München**
Luftgau VII	Gen.Maj. Zenetti	München
Luftgau XII	Oberst Heilingbrunner	Wiesbaden
Luftgau XIII	Oberst Musshoff	Nürnberg
5.Fliegerdivision	Gen.Maj. Ritter von Greim	
6.Fliegerdivision	Gen.Maj. Dessloch	
Luftflottenkommando 4	**Gen.d.Fl. Löhr**	**Wien (Vienna)**
Luftgau VIII	Gen.Maj. Danckelmann	Breslau
Luftgau XVII	Gen.Maj. Hirschauer	Wien
Luftamt Prague	unknown	Prague

LEFT: Bf 109 Ds of I./JG 53 ready for take-off from Wiesbaden-Erbenheim airfield in April 1939. Shortly after this photo was taken, the aircraft were replaced by 'Emils'

May to August 1939

This re–organisation led to yet another major redesignation of *Luftwaffe* units in May 1939. The old three-figure unit identifications were replaced by a one- or two-figure number. Units numbered between 1 and 25 were placed under the control of *Luftflotte 1* or *Luftwaffenkommando Ostpreussen*, those numbered between 26 and 50 were under *Luftflotte 2*, those between 51 and 75 under *Luftflotte 3* and those between 76 and 99 under *Luftflotte 4*. At the same time *Schwere Jagdgruppen* were redesignated *Zerstörergruppen* (destroyer groups) in preparation for their re-equipment with the twin-engined Bf 110.

Old Designation	Base	New designation	Base
Luftwaffe Lehrdivision			
I.(*leicht* J)/LG 2	Garz	I.(J)/LG 2	Garz
I.(*schwere* J)/LG 1	Barth	I.(Z)/LG 1	Barth
Luftflotte 1			
I./JG 130	Jesau	I./JG 1	Jesau
I./JG 131 'Richthofen'	Döberitz	I./JG 2 'Richthofen'	Döberitz
II./JG 231	Zerbst	I./JG 3	Zerbst
I./JG 141	Damm	I./ZG 1	Damm
II./JG 141	Fürstenwalde	I./ZG 76	Pardubitz
I./JG 231	Bernburg	I./ZG 2	Bernburg
Luftflotte 2			
I./JG 132 'Schlageter'	Köln	I./JG 26 'Schlageter'	Köln
II./JG 132 'Schlageter'	Dortmund	II./JG 26 'Schlageter'	Dortmund
I./JG 142 'Horst Wessel'	Dortmund	I./ZG 26 'Horst Wessel'	Dortmund
II./JG 142 'Horst Wessel'	Werl	II./ZG 26 'Horst Wessel'	Werl
III./JG 142 'Horst Wessel'	Lippstadt	III./ZG 26 'Horst Wessel'	Lippstadt
Luftflotte 3			
I./JG 233	Bad Aibling	I./JG 51	Bad Aibling
I./JG 433	Böblingen	I./JG 52	Böblingen
I./JG 133	Wiesbaden	I./JG 53	Wiesbaden
II./JG 133	Mannheim	II./JG 53	Mannheim
I./JG 143	Illesheim	I./ZG 52	Illesheim
Luftflotte 4			
I./JG 134	Wien	I./JG 76	Wien
I./JG 331	Mährisch-Trübau	I./JG 77	Breslau
II./JG 333	Marienbad	II./JG 77	Pilsen
I./JG 333	Herzogenaurach	II./ZG 1	Fürstenwalde
I./JG 144	Gablingen	II./ZG 76	Gablingen
Marinefliegerverband			
6.(J)/*Trägergruppe* 186	Kiel	II./Tr.Gr.186	Kiel

LEFT: A Bf 109 C or D belonging to St.G 77 begins its takeoff run from Breslau–Schöngarten airfield on 1 July 1939. The aircraft was painted black–green (RLM 70) on the uppersurfaces with light–blue (RLM 65) underneath. The unit markings clearly shows the code 'S2' in red thinly outlined in white although the remaining two letters cannot be discerned although they also appear to be red and white with the spinner painted yellow. These Bf 109s were used to fly above the Ju 87 Stukas and used to direct the assault on targets.

RIGHT: A pair of Bf 109 Ds of 3./JG 21 in close formation. (see also page 208)

LEFT: Major Bernhard Woldenga and Hptm. Martin Mettig at the ceremonial creation of I./JG 21 at Jesau in East Prussia in mid-July 1939. The unit was formed by the splitting of Woldenga's I./JG 1, Mettig taking over the new Gruppe. Note the He 70 in the background.

During 1937 the *Luftwaffe* had begun flying experimental night fighter sorties, and, by late 1938 two specialised squadrons had been formed. These were 10.(N)/JG 132 *'Richthofen'* under *Hptm.* Albert Blumensaat based at Döberitz and equipped with the Ar 68 and 11.(N)/LG 2 under *Oblt.* Johannes Steinhoff at Köln-Ostheim. Like most other *Jagdwaffe* units of the time, both units were redesignated, the former becoming successively 10.(N)/JG 131 and 10.(N)/JG 2, the latter becoming 10.(N)/JG 26 on 1 June 1939.

Convinced of the need for a substantial night fighter force, the RLM issued an order on 24 June calling for the formation of several other such units. These were I./JG 20 at Döberitz (formed from a basis provided by I./JG 2), I./JG 21 at Jesau (formed from a basis of I./JG 1), 1. and 2./JG 70 and 1. and 2./JG 71 at Bad Aibling (formed from a basis of I./JG 51 and I./JG 52), 10./JG 72 at Mannheim (formed from a basis of II./JG 53) and 11./JG 72 at Böblingen (formed from a basis of I./JG 52). Apart from JG 72 which flew Ar 68s, the remaining units were equipped with the Bf 109 D or E. Changing requirements, probably dictated by the gathering of war clouds, led to all these units with the exception of 10. and 11./JG 72 being transferred to day fighter operations on 16 August 1939.

On 15 September, I./JG 70 under *Hptm.* Hans-Jürgen von Cramon Taubadel (to which a *3.Staffel* had been added) was redesignated I./JG 54, the new *Gruppe* being expanded to full *Geschwader* strength by July 1940. On 6 October, 1. and 2./JG 71, which also had a *3.Staffel* added equipped with Czech-built Avia B 534s, was incorporated into II./JG 51. Around the same time, 11./JG 72 (and possibly 1./JG 71) formed the basis of II./JG 52. The only *Staffeln* to remain as night fighter units were 10.(N)/JG 2, 10.(N)/JG 72 (which became 11.(N)/JG 2) and 10.(N)/JG 26 (which became 12.(N)/JG 2), the three *Staffeln* being collectively known as IV.(N)/JG 2. This *Gruppe* was eventually re-designated III./NJG 1.

Despite the intention to re-equip all the *Zerstörergruppen* with the Bf 110, only three units had received the twin-engined fighter when the Second World War broke out. These were I.(Z)/LG 1, I./ZG 1 and I./ZG 76, the other units retaining their Bf 109 Ds and Es. All the remaining units, with the exception of I. and II./ZG 26, received temporary fighter designations. Thus from September 1939 until the end of February 1940, II./ZG 1 was known as JGr 101 , I./ZG 2 as JGr 102, III./ZG 26 as JGr 126, I./ZG 52 as JGr 152 and II./ZG 76 and JGr 176.

May to August 1939

BELOW: This Bf 109 E of Stab I./JG 1, marked with a single black chevron and Jesau Kreuz badge, was photographed at Seerappen airfield during the summer of 1939. Although I./JG 1's main base was Jesau near Seerappen, the latter airfield was often used during the summer manoeuvres. The colour of the spinner indicated to which unit the aircraft belonged: green for the Stab and white, red and yellow for 1., 2. or 3.Staffel. This aircraft appears to be brand new and sports a splinter pattern camouflage of black-green (RLM 70) and dark-green (RLM 71) with light-blue (RLM 65) underneath. The demarcation line between the upper and lower colours on the engine and leading edge of the wings appear very sharp.

ABOVE: This Bf 109 E-1 'White 4' was photographed at Pardubitz, Czechoslovakia in May 1939 just after II./JG 141 was redesignated I./ZG 76. At this time, its Bf 109s carried the second Gruppe horizontal bar but, not long afterwards, I./ZG 76 received its first Bf 110s which carried the four character code system.

'Jesau Kreuz' of I./JG 1

BELOW: When I./JG 21 was formed from I./JG 1 in July 1939, the new Gruppe was equipped with Bf 109 Ds, the latter retaining its much more powerful 'Emils'. These photos show 'Yellow 2' of 3./JG 21 in flight.

BELOW: A pair of Bf 109 Es from the Stab II./ZG 1 (formerly I./JG 333) photographed at Friedeberg during the summer of 1939. Note that the staff symbols and horizontal bars were painted in white outlines only, not the more usual black.

May to August 1939

RIGHT: Bf 109 Es from I./JG 53, probably the first Staffel at Wiesbaden-Erbenheim during July 1939. 'White 2 and 3' can be identified in this photo. At this time airfield defence was not yet considered of any great importance as can be seen from the rudimentary anti-aircraft gun installation in the foreground.

BELOW: Another view of a Bf 109 E of 1./JG 53, 'White 11'. At this time most fighters were still finished in black-green (RLM 70) on the uppersurfaces with pale-blue (RLM 65) underneath. Note the Dornier Do 17 P in the background.

BELOW: A line-up of Bf 109 Es from 5./JG 52 at Böblingen airfield. This unit had originally been formed as 11./JG 72 on 11 July 1939, being renamed and re-equipped with the Bf 109 E in September. II./JG 52 remained at Böblingen until 31 October 1939, when it moved to Mannheim-Sandhofen. These aircraft still carry the early style markings including the Hakenkreuz carried over the fin and rudder.

RIGHT: A Bf 109 E of I./JG 52 taxiing along the grass at Mannheim–Sandhofen airfield. Note the Bf 109 E behind has light-blue (RLM 65 fuselage sides.

May to August 1939

One of the best Staffeln of the Luftwaffe.

WOLF-DIETRICH HUY

Lt. Wolf-Dietrich Huy of 6./Tr.Gr. 186 was later awarded the Ritterkreuz before being captured by British forces in North Africa on 29 October 1942.

I was born on 2 August 1917 at Freiburg im Breisgau. Despite the fact that my father was a '*Forstmeister*' or Forestry Commissioner, I had always dreamt of going to sea after a friend of the family regaled me with passionate accounts of life in the Navy. I subsequently discovered that he had never been in the Navy, but he seemed able to find the words to excite my interest. Therefore, when I got my '*Abitur*'[1] in Easter 1935, I decided to join the Navy. I received two and half months preliminary instruction before transferring to a sail training ship. After that I spent eight months sailing around the world as a cadet aboard the cruiser 'Karlsruhe'. After returning, I undertook more courses but, in 1937, it was explained that only twenty per cent of the 200 cadets of which I was one, could stay in the Navy. The remaining eighty per cent would be transferred to another part of the armed forces, most probably the army, or perhaps the Luftwaffe which had recently been reborn. At that time, Germany's unemployment rate was still high and the authorisation to study at high school was rarely given. It seemed that my future lay in the armed forces, and if not in the Navy, then perhaps the *Luftwaffe*.

In the meantime, I heard that the Navy was looking for sea observers. I applied, one of about 200 applicants, and we began training in this role. The arrangement was that we were to be trained and used as observers during the following four years, and after that returned to the Navy. This happened to most of my comrades. Virtually all of them went back to the Navy, many to be commissioned as *U-Boot* commanders, but a large number were killed or reported missing in action at sea.

A few of us like myself were unsatisfied with being merely observers, and we decided to opt for the *Luftwaffe* in order to become pilots. This meant abandoning our naval uniforms and buying ourselves new ones in *Luftwaffe* blue.

From 16 March 1939 until end of that month, we received our '*Jagdvorkurs*' (preliminary fighter training) at Bug auf Rügen, before being posted to the famous fighter school at Werneuchen. We began by flying the Ar 65 (with which we were already familiar) and the Go 145 and Fw 56 with the aim of being prepared to pilot the Bf 109. On 16 June 1939, I made over fifteen take-offs and flights in a Bf 108 with *Oblt*. Wilhelm Hachfeld as my instructor. Next day, I flew the Bf 109 for the first time. I also learned blind flying and to pilot larger aircraft including the three-engined Ju 52. (*Note: His teacher at this time was Oblt. Rolf Kaldrack, who, like Huy, had joined the Navy but chose to transfer to the Luftwaffe in 1935. He had become an ace during the Spanish Civil War*).

On 1 July 1939, I was posted to II./*Trägergruppe* 186 at Kiel-Holtenau. There I met at least five other former naval officers (I had the rank of *Leutnant* at the end of my time with the Navy). We soon understood why so many officers with naval experience were chosen to man the unit. Several years before, the Reich had begun the construction of an aircraft carrier, and we had been chosen to pilot its aeroplanes. Although launched on 8 December 1938, the carrier was far from being completed, and we were forced to train using an artificial landing strip with the same dimensions as that planned for her flight deck. At that time we mostly flew the He 50, a biplane which was intended to be used from the carrier as dive-bomber.

Our carrier training did not last long, and following the outbreak of the Second World War, we were posted to Jever in order to protect the German Bight. Most of the capital ships of the *Kriegsmarine* were anchored in this area, and were extremely vulnerable to RAF bombing attacks.

At this time we began exchanging our old Bf 109 '*Bertas*' for new '*Emils*'. The *Emil* was not much different to fly from the *Berta*. The main difference was the engine which was much more powerful. At the end of November 1939, our unit was transferred to Nordholz, where the fighter commander in the area, *Major* Carl Schumacher, seemed to have forgotten that we were combat ready. So we were not informed of the British raids on the German Bight!

In March 1940, our 5./*Trägergruppe* 186 was moved to the island of Wangerooge, still with the aim of protecting the German Bight against RAF attack. The tiny windswept island off the German North Sea coast made take-offs and landings quite difficult... but the training we had received during the exercises on the artificial landing strip made us one of the best *Staffeln* of the *Luftwaffe* at this manoeuvre.

1. *Abitur* = a school-leaving exam qualifying for admission to university.

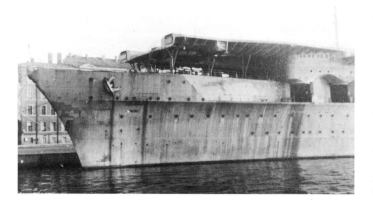

LEFT AND RIGHT: The aircraft carrier Graf Zeppelin was laid down at Kiel in 1935 and although launched on 8 December 1938 the ship was never completed. It was designed to have a displacement of 19,250 tons and a speed of 32 knots with a main armament of sixteen 150 mm (5.9 inch) guns and ten 105 mm (4.1 inch) guns. Her flightdeck measured 240 metres (88.5 ft) and a provision was made for 40 aircraft, 28 Ju 87 Cs and 12 Bf 109 Ts.

May to August 1939

Luftwaffe Fighter strength and serviceability
August 1939

Luftwaffe Lehrdivision

I.(Z)/LG 1	Bf 110 C	Barth	32	(29)
Stab LG 2	Bf 109 E	Jüterbog	3	(3)
I.(J)/LG 2	Bf 109 E	Garz	36	(34)
10.(N)/JG 26	Bf 109 D	Köln-Ostheim	10	(9)

Luftflotte 1

I./JG 1	Bf 109 E	Jesau	54	(54)
I./JG 26	Bf 109 E	Köln	48	(48)
II./JG 26	Bf 109 E	Düsseldorf	48	(44)
I./ZG 26	Bf 109 D	Dortmund	52	(46)
II./ZG 26	Bf 109 D	Werl	48	(47)
III./ZG 26	Bf 109 D	Lippstadt	48	(44)

Luftflotte 2

I./JG 2	Bf 109 E	Döberitz	42	(39)
10.(N)/JG 2	Bf 109 D	Döberitz	9	(9)
Stab JG 3	Bf 109 E	Bernburg	3	(3)
I./JG 3	Bf 109 E	Zerbst	48	(42)
I./JG 20	Bf 109 E	Döberitz	21	(20)
I./JG 21	Bf 109 D	Jesau	29	(28)
I./ZG 1	Bf 110 C	Damm	32	(24)
II./ZG 1	Bf 109 E	Fürstenwalde	36	(36)
I./ZG 2	Bf 109 D	Bernburg	44	(40)

Luftflotte 3

I./JG 51	Bf 109 E	Bad Aibling	47	(39)
I./JG 52	Bf 109 E	Böblingen	39	(34)
I./JG 53	Bf 109 E	Wiesbaden	51	(39)
II./JG 53	Bf 109 E	Mannheim	43	(41)
1. & 2./JG 70	Bf 109 D	Herzogenaurach	24	(24)
1./JG 71	Bf 109 D	Böblingen	15	(12)
2./JG 71	Bf 109 D	Fürstenfeldbruck	24	(6)
10.(N)/JG 72	Ar 68 F	Mannheim	6	(12)
11.(N)/JG 72	Ar 68 F	Böblingen	12	(12)
I./ZG 52	Bf 109 D	Illesheim	44	(43)

Luftflotte 4

I./JG 76	Bf 109 E	Wien-Aspern	49	(45)
I./JG 77	Bf 109 E	Breslau	50	(43)
II./JG 77	Bf 109 E	Pilsen	50	(36)
I./ZG 76	Bf 110 C	Olmütz	31	(29)
II./ZG 76	Bf 109 D	Gablingen	40	(39)

Marinefliegerverbänd

II.(J)/186	Bf 109 B/E	Kiel-Holtenau	24	(24)

Totals by functions of all aircraft

Single engined day fighters	771 (676)
Heavy day fighters	408 (377)

BELOW: A Bf 109 C or D of Stab I./JG 20 which was established at Berlin-Döberitz on 15 July 1939 but did not receive its first aircraft, a small number of Bf 109 C 'Caesar', until August of that year. Although designated I./JG 20, some of the unit's aircraft carried the white vertical bar marking indicating a third Gruppe. The unit was eventually officially redesignated III./JG 51 on 4 July 1940, but this was obviously long after its formation. Superimposed on the cross-bow, which was a derivative of the 'bow and arrow' emblem of 1./JG 20, is a personal insignia of a running hare. The aircraft is painted black-green (RLM 70) on the uppersurfaces and light blue (RLM 65) underneath. The spinner forward of the rear ring appears to be yellow (RLM 04).

May to August 1939

ABOVE: A mechanic working on a Bf 109 E of 2./JG 3 with the bell emblem of the Sudeten-Deutsch Partei painted under the cockpit. Note the Bf 109 in the background, 'Red 10', which carries the new style cross with wide white angles on the fuselage which has pale blue (RLM 65) sides. The Bf 109 in front still carries the dark camouflage of black-green (RLM 70) on the uppersurfaces.

BELOW: Uffz. Emil Omert of 2./JG 3 poses in front of his Bf 109 E coded 'Red 6' of 2./JG 3 at Döberitz or Zerbst, late summer 1939. Omert, who was later to be awarded the Ritterkreuz, was posted to a Luftkriegschule shortly afterwards where he was promoted to a Leutnant. In April 1940, he was transferred to JG 77. Note the Sudeten-Deutsch Partei badge of 2./JG 3 below the cockpit.

2./JG 3 badge denoting the 'Sudeten-Deutsch Partei'

Messerschmitt Bf 109 E-1 of 2./JG 3 at Zerbst, winter 1939-1940
It was not unusual for Bf 109s of the early war period to have an overall black-green (RLM 70) on the uppersurfaces with light blue (RLM 65) underneath. This aircraft carries the bell emblem of the Sudeten-Deutsch Partei (German Sudeten Party) which was adopted by 2./JG 3.

ABOVE, ABOVE LEFT AND LEFT: These photos show damaged Bf 109 Es of JGr 101 (a temporary redesignation of II./ZG 1) taken around late August 1939 in northern Germany, at either Schleswig or Neumünster. As this evidence shows the Bf 109 was not an easy aircraft to fly.

RIGHT: A Bf 109 E -1 of the Stab II./ZG 1 photographed during the summer of 1939. This unit was formed from I./JG 333 on 12 May 1939 at Fürstenwalde and was equipped with the Bf 109 E-1. The significance of the white rectangle on the cowling is not known.

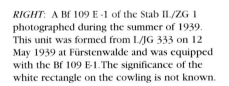

LEFT: Another view of the Bf 109 E -1 of II./ZG 1 showing the early type Balkenkreuz with narrow white outline on the fuselage sides and beneath the wings. The aircraft was finished in black-green (RLM 70) on the uppersurfaces and light-blue (RLM 65) underneath. This machine also shows the hard demarcation line on the nose to the leading edge of the wing between the upper and lower colour which also appears on the aircraft of ZG 1 top left. It is probable that this batch of Bf 109s left the factory finished in this way.

May to August 1939

ABOVE AND BELOW: Taken after making a belly landing at Seerappen airfield in East Prussia in August 1939, this Bf 109 E-3 was operated by 1./JG 1. Note the Gruppe emblem, the 'Jesau Kreuz' beneath the cockpit, the white number '6' and the white spinner.

RIGHT: This Bf 109 D-1 carried the red and white 'Shark's Teeth' insignia of II./ZG 76 which was temporarily redesignated JGr 176 during the winter of 1939-40. The unit retained the marking when it was re-equipped with the Bf 110 twin-engined fighter.

Messerschmitt Bf 109 D-1, 2./JGr 176, Gablingen, August 1939

For a short period, II./ZG 76, the 'Haifisch Gruppe', was known as JGr 176 pending its re-equipment with the Bf 110. Its Bf 109 Ds carried red and white 'Shark's Teeth' on their noses, this marking becoming much better known after the unit received its Bf 110s. The aircraft was painted in a splinter pattern of black-green and dark green (RLM 70 and 71) on the uppersurfaces with light blue (RLM 65) underneath.

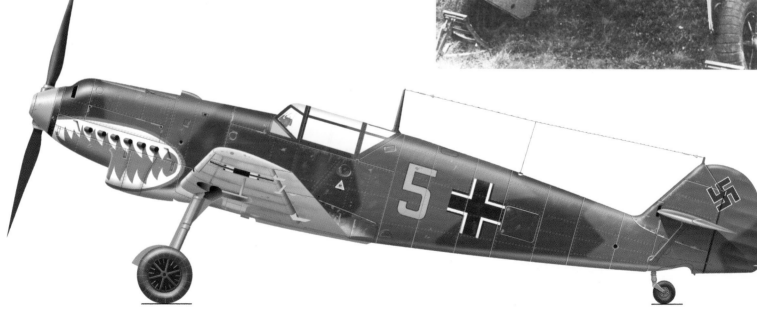

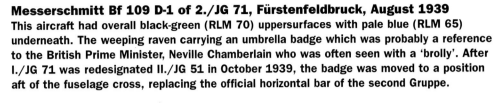

May to August 1939

Messerschmitt Bf 109 D-1 of 2./JG 71, Fürstenfeldbruck, August 1939
This aircraft had overall black-green (RLM 70) uppersurfaces with pale blue (RLM 65) underneath. The weeping raven carrying an umbrella badge which was probably a reference to the British Prime Minister, Neville Chamberlain who was often seen with a 'brolly'. After I./JG 71 was redesignated II./JG 51 in October 1939, the badge was moved to a position aft of the fuselage cross, replacing the official horizontal bar of the second Gruppe.

**JG 71
(later II./JG 51)
'weeping raven'
The colours of the
bird and
positioning of the
badge could vary**

ABOVE AND RIGHT: At the beginning of September 1939, 2./JG 71 moved to Fürstenfeldbruck airfield to protect Munich against possible reprisal raids for the attack on Poland. These Bf 109 Ds, coded 'Red 6", above, and 'Red 11', right, carried an emblem of a weeping raven with an umbrella, often purported to be a characature of the British Prime Minister, Neville Clamberlain. It was introduced before the outbreak of war with Britain and France on 3 September. 2./JG 71 was soon to form the basis of II./JG 51.

LEFT: A Schwarm of four Bf 109 E including 'White 15, 7 and 4' from 1./JG 51 photographed at Eutingen airfield in August-September 1939. This was shortly after the Gruppe had moved from Bad Aibling. Note that the unit's emblem does not appear on this side of these aircraft.

May to August 1939

ABOVE: A Rotte of Bf 109 Ds from I./JG 71 take off from Fürstenfeldbruck on a training flight. The aircraft were marked 'Red 12 and 5' respectively and both carried the badge depicting a 'weeping raven carrying an umbrella', no doubt in reference to the British Prime Minister at that time, Neville Chamberlain. The badge was later adopted by II./JG 51 in October 1939 when the unit was redesignated and the badge moved to a position aft of the fuselage cross.

RIGHT AND BELOW: These Bf 109 Es from 6./JG 26 were photographed in Düsseldorf in the summer of 1939. They both cary the JG 26 'Schlageter' badge and also the 'Steinbock' (Ram) badge. The aircraft on the right is 'Yellow 14' and the one below 'Yellow 7" both sets of numbers were thinly outlined in black. They were camouflaged in a splinter pattern of black-green (RLM 70) and dark green (RLM 71) with light blue (RLM 65) underneath. The cowling on the aircraft below also shows yellow (RLM 04) gun troughs. Previous to May 1939 the unit designation was 6./JG 132. Shortly after these photos were taken the unit moved to Bönninghardt on 25 August 1939 a just a few days before the outbreak of the war. At this time the Staffelkapitän was Oblt. Alfred Pomaska.

The 'Steinbock' (Ram) badge of 6./JG 26

LEFT AND BELOW: Bf 109 E, W.Nr.782, coded 'White 4' and 'White 15' of 4./JG 26. This was the original 'Adamsonstaffel' which was redesignated 8./JG 26 on 23 September 1939. Note that 'White 4' also has yellow (RLM 04) gun troughs.

BELOW: A group of Bf 109 Es from 6./JG 26 photographed at Düsseldorf airfield on 10 August 1939, just before the outbreak of the Second World War. The aircraft in the foreground has white wing-tips and a white tail, a marking adopted for manoeuvres which were carried out at the time. The aircraft carried yellow numbers (RLM 27) thinly outlined in black.

JG 26 'Schlageter' badge

Messerschmitt Bf 109 E-1 of 6./JG 26, summer 1939
For the manoeuvres held during the summer of 1939, the tails and wing-tips of some of II./JG 26's aircraft were painted white. The 'Schlageter' badge was carried on both sides of the fuselage of the unit's Bf 109s. The aircraft was camouflaged in a splinter pattern of black-green and dark green (RLM 70 and 71) on the uppersurfaces with pale-blue (RLM 65) underneath.

May to August 1939

LEFT: The Kommandeur of I./JG 26, Hptm. Gotthard Handrick standing on the wing of his Bf 109 E-1 at Köln during the summer of 1939. As well as the JG 26 badge, Handrick's aircraft carried another variant of the 'top hat' emblem originally used by 2.J/88 in Spain which he re-introduced into JG 26.

BELOW: A complete side view of Hptm. Gotthard Handrick's Bf 109 E-1 of I./JG 26 which carried the double chevron marking of a Gruppenkommandeur. It also has the famous script 'S' badge of the 'Schlageter' Geschwader. Handrick had gained the Pentathlon Gold Medal at the 1936 Berlin Olympic Games.

The oil filler point was situated on the port side on all Bf 109s. The coloured triangle was brown (RLM 26) outlined in white with the word 'Rotring' (a trademark of 'Red Ring' lubrication oil) written inside. The two red (RLM 23) rings underneath were not always applied.

Messerschmitt Bf 109 E-1, Gruppenkommandeur Hptm. Gotthard Handrick, I./JG 26, Köln summer 1939
This aircraft was painted in a splinter pattern of black-green (RLM 70) and dark green (RLM 71) on the uppersurfaces with light blue (RLM 65) underneath.

Detail of Oblt. Handrick's version of the 'top hat' badge as shown on his Bf 109 E-1

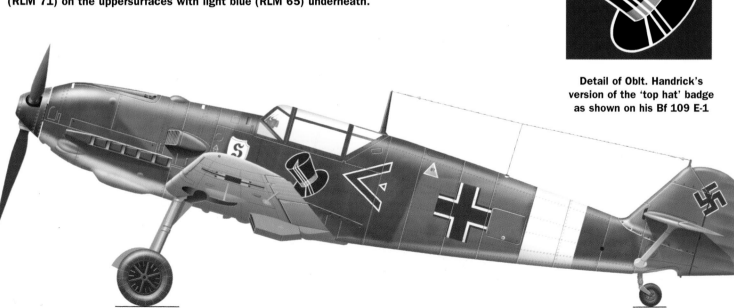

The Kunstflugstaffel The Luftwaffe Aerobatic Team 1938-1939

The 'Kunstflugstaffel' was formed initially to take part in the large military air show in Arlon, Belgium in 1938 to show off the new Luftwaffe's flying skills. The unit went on to participate in several further air displays in front to other foreign national dignitaries.

LEFT: Hptm. Hanns Trübenbach checks out the field prior to a flight with Bü 133 Jungmeisters in the background.

BELOW: Five of the Kunstflugstaffel's Bücker Jungmeisters performing part of their aerobatic routine.

BELOW: Nine aircraft of the Luftwaffe Kunstflugstaffel, with the three lead aircraft trailing smoke, perform a formation loop. The unit's aircraft were finished in pale silver grey overall with an emerald green striped flash on the fuselage.

BELOW: During the summer of 1938, Hptm. Hanns Trübenbach of I.(J)/LG 2 took the twelve best pilots from his unit to create the Luftwaffe Kunstflugstaffel. The unit was equipped with nine Bü 133 Jungmeister (Young Champion) trainers, one of the finest aerobatic aircraft of its generation. Aircraft were finished pale grey (RLM 63) overall with a distinctive green stripe along the fuselage.

BELOW: Pilots of the Kunstflugstaffel stand in front of two of their Bü 133s at Brussels-Evere on 8 July 1939. From left to right are: Oblt. Gerhard Homuth, Lt. Hans-Wedige von Weiher, Lt. Herbert Ihlefeld, Lt. Georg Graner, Hptm. Joachim Wille (who was killed in a crash later in the day), Ofw. Hermann Staege, Uffz. Josef Heinzeller, Ofw. Siegfried Krause, Ofw. Erwin Clausen, and a Belgian officer.

We were to be known officially as 'The Luftwaffe Aerobatics Team'!

HANNS TRÜBENBACH

Hanns Trübenbach commanded I./LG 2 during the Polish campaign in 1939 and in August, 1940 was appointed Kommodore of JG 52. He was wounded over London in October of that year, but survived the war.

I was born on 26 March 1906 in Chemnitz. I started flying in 1926 at Leipzig/Mockau with the intention of becoming a civilian pilot. I obtained my first certificate in the autumn of that year at Leipzig/Mokau. I then went to the *Verkehrsfliegerschule* at Stettin where I flew Fokker civilian aircraft. Following Stettin, I attended a large civilian pilots school[1] at Berlin-Staaken which was headed by a former bomber commander from the First World War, *Major* Keller. At this school, I was given further training and attained several more certificates including one for aerobatics which I had performed at Schleissheim. I also received instruction on fighter aircraft as well as seaplanes. Following several months spent on a boat with the Navy, I became a civilian pilot with *Lufthansa* and then later with the Fokker Company. By the time Hitler came to power and began to rebuild the *Luftwaffe*, I was a qualified blind-flying instructor. When my uncle - a general - heard of the call for pilots for the new *Luftwaffe*, he recommended that I volunteer and I found myself in the first batch of 25 pilots - among them, a few former airline pilots like myself - which would form the nucleus of the new *Luftwaffe*. I met Adolf Galland and a few younger pilots who I already knew as well as some 'older' pilots. We attended the military academy and at one stage my teacher was Erwin Rommel, who in the future would become famous in Africa as the 'Desert Fox'.

I decided that I wanted to become a fighter pilot and in June 1935, I was posted to the north coast of Germany in order to set up a *'See-Jagdgruppe'* (Marine Fighter Group) which would eventually become known as *Küstenjagdstaffel* 136 based at Kiel-Holtenau. We were equipped with the Heinkel He 51 and the unit steadily grew in strength. In October 1936, our unit was designated I./JG 136 and I was appointed its *Staffelkapitän*.

As was the case with all *Luftwaffe* units in Germany at that time, mine continually and quickly expanded in size and strength and my *Gruppe* was split to form a new unit, I./LG 2, which I was ordered to command.

In the spring of 1938, I heard from a Hungarian air force pilot that a large military air show was due to be held at Arlon in Belgium and that it was thought that German pilots should be seen there. I was very excited at this prospect and I immediately began to train for this event, together with two other pilots from my *Gruppe*, *Lt.* Gerhard Homuth (who would become a future *Luftwaffe* fighter ace with 63 victories and who would be awarded the *Ritterkreuz*, serving as Kommandeur of both I./JG 27 and I./JG 54) and *Lt.* Georg Graner. We received unofficial sanction to call ourselves 'The *Luftwaffe* Aerobatic Team' and were allowed to go to Belgium to perform with a *Kette* of Bücker 133 'Jungmeisters.

We proved so successful in this venture - this was May 1938 - that upon our return to Germany we were immediately contacted by a high-ranking officer and were told that we were now to be known officially as 'The *Luftwaffe* Aerobatics Team'! In August, we had an opportunity to put on a show for a visiting French general and his staff using our complete *'Staffel'*. Our pilots were, without exception, excellent and some of them would embark on very successful flying and service careers during the forthcoming war: *Hptm.* Joachim Wille, *Ofw.* Erwin Clausen, *Ofw.* Siegfried Krause, *Lt.* Hans-Wedige von Weiher, *Ofw.* Hermann Staege, *Uffz.* Josef Heinzeller and *Lt.* Herbert Ihlefeld (who would act as a reserve pilot) would all join our team. Apart from Homuth, Clausen would have an impressive career, scoring 132 victories and becoming *Kommandeur* I./JG 11. He was eventually awarded the *Ritterkreuz* and *Eichenlaub*. Herbert Ihlefeld also achieved 130 victories and was awarded the *Ritterkreuz* with *Eichenlaub* and *Schwertern*.

We trained for several hours every day and formulated new group display formations, discussing our methods over and over again. We developed special codes which we would use in the air to simultaneously start new formations. We had no radios on board our aircraft and I had to signal with my arms in different ways to give the start signal for all the different manoeuvres. My men very quickly adapted themselves to my way of thinking and to my flying style and were able, in seconds, to commence any type of manoeuvre which I specified. The truth was that we were becoming the best pilots in the *Luftwaffe* - and all of us were fighter pilots.

Our greatest show was to be our last. It was no surprise to be invited to attend a large show held at Brussels/Evere on 7 July 1939 where we would 'confront' the best teams from France and England under the watchful eyes of 100,000 spectators, including many high ranking officers and King Leopold III of Belgium. *Generaloberst* Milch, the Secretary of State for Aviation, had also travelled from Germany to attend and he gave me a few words of encouragement before our performance.

Up we went and everything was going well; we flew in at 50 metres from a corner to approach the VIP stand. We also managed some beautiful formation flying but on our return, *Hptm.* Wille's '7' hit some turbulence and he lost control of his aircraft. He crashed and was so badly injured that he died minutes later. Milch stood up on the VIP stand with a livid expression on his face - he was certain that it was '1' that had crashed (my aircraft) and not '7'.

Thus the show ended in tragedy and we flew back to Germany. Of course, we subsequently discussed what had happened many times but I was heartened that not one of my pilots had been discouraged by what had happened. However, from another viewpoint, I was beginning to wonder whether my team would exist for much longer; we were members of the *Luftwaffe*, not civilians, and were aware that our country was preparing for 'something big' which would happen at some time over the next few months.

We were, indeed, all posted back to our unit, I.(J)/LG 2 and I re-took command. It was July 1939 and the 'something big' was not that far away...

---

1. This was the DVS (Deutsche Verkehrsflieger–Schule) at Staaken, a civilian establishment which was set up with the objective of providing a uniform standard of C-grade training.

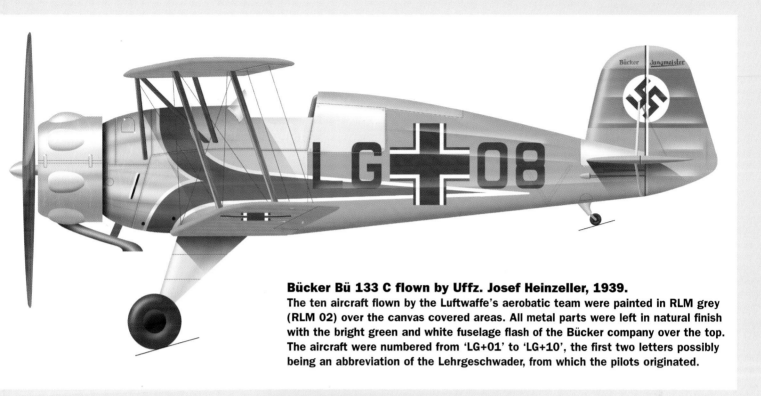

Bücker Bü 133 C flown by Uffz. Josef Heinzeller, 1939.
The ten aircraft flown by the Luftwaffe's aerobatic team were painted in RLM grey (RLM 02) over the canvas covered areas. All metal parts were left in natural finish with the bright green and white fuselage flash of the Bücker company over the top. The aircraft were numbered from 'LG+01' to 'LG+10', the first two letters possibly being an abbreviation of the Lehrgeschwader, from which the pilots originated.

RIGHT: Uffz. Josef Heinzeller of the Luftwaffe Kunstflugstaffel (Air Force Aerobatic Team) poses on the wing of his Bü 133 C Jungmeister trainer. The aircraft was finished in pale grey overall with a green stripe edged in white painted along the fuselage sides.

BELOW: Karl Helmer standing in front of a similarly marked Bü 133s as the Kunstflugstaffel. He was 'Europa Kunstflugmeister' (European Aerobatic Champion).

RIGHT: Herbert Ihlefeld (wearing the Spanienkreuz on his breast pocket) explains to his commanding officer, Hanns Trübenbach, the details of a possible manoeuvre to be attempted by the Kunststaffel. At this time, Ihlefeld was Adjutant in I.(J)/LG 2 and a reserve pilot in the aerobatic team. He later went on to command JG 52, JG 11 and JG 1.

September 1939

ABOVE: Hitler studying a plan of campaign on 12 September 1939 during the attack on Poland.

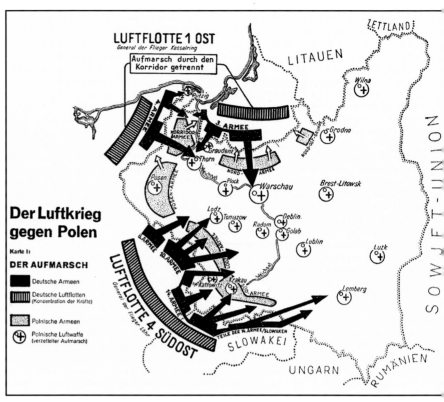

ABOVE: 'The Air War against Poland': A contemporary German map of the time showing the dispositions of the German and Polish armies and air forces.

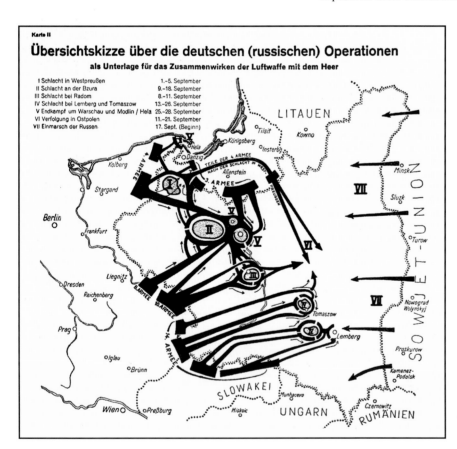

ABOVE: 'An Overview of the German (Russian) Operations': Another contemporary German map of the time showing the air war on Poland and the various stages reached at specific dates. Note that the Russians are included in the operations, since they invaded Poland from the east starting on the 17 September 1939.

BELOW: A line-up of Bf 109 Es from 1.(J)/LG 2 ready for operations at Bromberg airfield in September 1939. The aircraft in the foreground 'White 1' belonged to the Staffelkapitän, Oblt. Hans-Erwin Jäger.

The Invasion of Poland

Convinced that Britain would not honour its treaty with Poland, Hitler fixed the invasion for 03.00 hours on 26 August 1939. Then, on 25 August, Hitler learned that the British Foreign Secretary, Lord Halifax, and the Polish ambassador in London, Count Edward Raczynski, had signed a mutual assistance pact. The German leader immediately ordered the planned invasion to be halted to give him time to review the situation. Hitler then received the British Ambassador to Berlin, Sir Neville Henderson, and offered to guarantee the security of the British Empire if she would stay at peace.

Henderson then flew to London, returning to Berlin with Chamberlain's reply on 28 August. The reply stated that Britain refused to countenance any proposal that would jeopardise the independence of a state to which it had given its firm guarantee, but suggested that Germany and Poland should enter into direct negotiations. Hitler finally agreed to meet a Polish representative on 30 August, but in his own mind this was merely to receive a one-man surrender deputation. Despite these efforts and those by Mussolini a day later, Hitler had already decided to go to war. At 17.00 hours on 31 August the order was given to *General* Gerd von Rundstedt to unleash the attack on Poland which would begin at dawn on the following day.

Late in 1938, an Air Force staff had been established in Poland, the new group being charged with the creation of a defensive organisation to combat the overwhelming and technical superiority of any potential aggressors. At this time, the only fighters available to the Polish Air Force were the obsolete PZL P-7 and P-11. Both were designed by *Ing.* Zygmunt Pulawski and were high gull-wing monoplanes with fixed undercarriages. The P-7 was powered by a 585 hp Bristol Jupiter VII F radial engine and some 150 aircraft were completed before production switched to the P-11. This was powered by a 645 hp Bristol Mercury engine which gave it a maximum speed of 390 km/h (242 mph) at 5,500 m (18,000 ft) - some 160 km/h (100 mph) slower than the Bf 109 E.

ABOVE: A Poli*sh* PZL P-23b Karas reconnaissance aircraft preparing for take off. A total of 205 of these two-seat aircraft were available to the Polish Air Force at the time of the German invasion.

BELOW: The commander in chief of the Luftwaffe, Reichsmarschall Hermann Göring inspects a group of personnel just prior to the Polish campaign. These visits were used as morale boosters for the troops and were often accompanied by award ceremonies.

When the invasion began at 04.45 hours on 1 September 1939, the Polish Air Force (PLW) had an operational personnel strength of 7,649 officers and men and a total of 841 aircraft (including a front line strength of 30 P-7 and 130 P-11 fighters, 114 P-23 bomber-reconnaissance aircraft and 36 P-37, 49 R-XIII and 35 RWD-14 army co-operation aircraft), the rest were either training, reserve or in repair, plus 16 floatplanes. With a four to one numerical superiority and a vastly better technical ability, *Luftwaffe* forces, drawn mainly from *Luftflotten* 1 and 4, were able to virtually destroy the Polish Air Force at one stroke. By the second day of the invasion, few Polish fighters were still serviceable, and ten days later organised resistance by the PLW had virtually come to an end. Warsaw finally surrendered on 27 September. Total losses suffered by the Polish Air Force were 90% of its equipment and 70% of its personnel. Like the Czechs before them, the remaining Polish pilots made their way to France and Britain where they joined and fought in the Air Forces of these countries.

Single engined fighter units operating over Poland included I.(J)/LG 2, I./JG 1, I./JG 21, I./JG 76, I./JG 77, II.(J)/186(T), II./ZG 1 and JGr 102 (later I./ZG 2). Despite the success of Luftwaffe operations, relatively few sorties were in fact flown by these units, the new Bf 110 destroyer shouldering most of the burden of bomber escort and ground strafing. The highest scoring German fighter pilot of the campaign was Hptm. Hannes Gentzen the Kommandeur of JGr 102. He scored his first victory on 2 September followed by others on the 3rd and the 13th, (two PZL P-11 fighters and a P-37 bomber), and destroyed a further nine on the ground. On the 14th, he shot down four PZL P-23s and was later awarded the Iron Cross First Class. Another successful unit was I./JG 21 which claimed six victories during the campaign.

September 1939

Jagdwaffe Order of Battle – 1 September 1939

Luftflotte 1   General der Flieger Albert Kesselring

1.Fliegerdivision Generalleutnant Ulrich Grauert

1.(J)/LG 2	Bf 109 E	Malzow	*Major* Hanns Trübenbach
2. & 3.(J)/LG 2	Bf 109 E	Lottin	*Major* Hanns Trübenbach
I./ZG 1	Bf 110 C	Mühlen	*Major* Joachim Friedrich Huth
JGr 101 (II./ZG 1)	Bf 109 E	Lichtenau	*Major* Reichardt

Luftwaffenlehrdivision Generalmajor Förster

I.(Z)/LG 1	Bf 110 C	Jesau	*Major* Walter Grabmann

Luftwaffenkommando Ostpreussen Generalleutnant Wilhelm Wimmer

I./JG 1	Bf 109 E	Allenstein	*Hptm.* Bernhard Woldenga
I./JG 21	Bf 109 D	Gutenfeld	*Hptm.* Martin Mettig

Luftgau III (Berlin)

Stab JG 2	Bf 109 E	Döberitz	*Oberst* Gerd von Massow
I./JG 2	Bf 109 E	Döberitz	*Obstlt.* Carl Viek
10.(N)/JG 2	Bf 109 D	Straussberg	*Major* Albert Blumensaat

Luftgau IV (Dresden)

Stab JG 3	Bf 109 E	Zerbst	*Obstlt.* Max Ibel
I./JG 3	Bf 109 E	Brandis	*Obstlt.* Wolf-Heinrich von Houwald
I./JG 20	Bf 109 E	Sprottau	*Major* Siegfried Lehmann

Luftflotte 2   General der Flieger Hellmuth Felmy

Luftgau XI (Hannover)

II./JG 77	Bf 109 E	Nordholz	*Major* Carl Schumacher [1]
II.(J)/186	Bf 109 B/E	Kiel-Holtenau	*Hptm.* Heinrich Seeliger
Stab ZG 26	Bf 109 D	Varel	*Oberst* Kurt von Döring
I./ZG 26	Bf 109 D	Varel	*Obstlt.* Hermann Frommholz
JGr 126 (III./ZG 26)	Bf 109 D	Neumünster	*Hptm.* Johannes Schalk

Luftgau VI (Münster)

11.(N)/LG 2	Bf 109 D	Köln-Ostheim	
I./JG 52	Bf 109 E	Wittlich	*Hptm.*Dietrich von Pfeil und Klein Ellguth
II./ZG 26	Bf 109 D	Werl	*Major* Friedrich Vollbracht
Stab JG 26	Bf 109 E	Obendorf	*Obstlt.* Eduard von Schleich
I./JG 26	Bf 109 E	Obendorf	*Major* Gotthard Handrick
II./JG 26	Bf 109 E	Bönninghardt	*Hptm.* Herwig Knüppel

Luftflotte 3   General der Flieger Hugo Sperrle

Fliegerdivision 5 Generalmajor Robert von Greim

JGr 152 (I./ZG 52)	Bf 109 D	Biblis	*Hptm.* Karl-Heinz Lessmann

Fliegerdivision 6 Generalmajor Otto Dessloch

JGr 176 (II./ZG 76)	Bf 109 D	Gablingen	

Luftgau VII (München)

I./JG 51	Bf 109 E	Eutingen	*Hptm.* Hans-Heinrich Brustellin
I./JG 71	Bf 109 D	Fürstenfeldbruck	*Oblt.* Heinz Schumann
10.& 11.(N)/JG 72	Ar 68 F	Böblingen	

Luftgau XII (Wiesbaden)

Stab JG 53	Bf 109 E	Wiesbaden	*Oberst* Werner Junck
I./JG 53	Bf 109 E	Kirchberg	*Hptm.* Lothar von Janson
II./JG 53	Bf 109 E	Mannheim	*Major* Hubertus Merhardt von Bernegg

Luftgau XIII (Nürnberg)

1. & 2./JG 70	Bf 109 D	Herzogenaurach	*Hptm.* Hans-Jürgen von Cramon Taubadel

Luftflotte 4   General der Flieger Alexander Lohr

Fliegerführer zbV

Stab LG 2	Bf 109 E	Nieder-Ellguth	*Oberst* Baier
JGr 102 (I./ZG 2)	Bf 109 D	Gross-Stein	*Hptm.* Hans Gentzen

Luftgau VIII (Breslau

I./JG 76	Bf 109 E	Stubendorf	*Hptm.* Wilfried Müller-Rienzburg
I./JG 77	Bf 109 E	Juliusberg-Nord	*Hptm.* Johannes Janke

1. Schumacher was replaced by Major Harry von Bülow–Bothkamp on 12 November, Schumacher then becoming Geschwaderkommodore of JG 1

**1./ZG 2 and later
1./JGr 102
'Black Hand' badge**

Messerschmitt Bf 109 D-1 of 1./ZG 2, Summer 1939
1./ZG 2 which had been formed from 1./JG 231 by way of 1./JG 137 and after 21 September 1939 was a temporary designation for 1./JGr 102. This particular aircraft had overall black-green (RLM 70) uppersurfaces with pale blue (RLM 65) beneath. The badge painted below the cockpit was the 'Bernburger Jäger' (the hunter from Bernburg) with a black hand badge of the 1. Staffel on the nose. The white rear fuselage band may have been an identity marking during manoeuvres

RIGHT: A mechanic has removed – and is working on – the radio equipment of this Bf 109 D-1 of I./ZG 2, later redesignated 1./JGr 102 on 21 September 1939. The aircraft carries the 'Bernburger Jäger' badge and the 'Black Hand' emblem painted on the forward part of the engine cowling indicates the aircraft belongs to 1.Staffel

BELOW: Another view of a Bf 109D-1 of I./ZG 2, which was one of the most successful fighter units in the Polish campaign.

BELOW: This Bf 109 D of I./ZG 2 shows the Gruppenkommandeur Hptm. Johannes Gentzen sat in the cockpit, with his chief mechanic Uffz. Lösche standing on the wing. Note the partially visible chevron and the sharp paint demarcation line on the leading edge of the wing. Many future Ritterkreuzträger flew with this unit, amongst them Lt. Adolf Galland (T.O. in 1936), Lt. Dietrich Hrabak (T.O. in 1937), Hptm. Max Ibel (Staffelkapitän of the 1.Staffel in 1936) and Lt. Gustav Rödel (a pilot in the 1.Staffel).

**I./ZG 2 and later JGr 102
'Bernburger Jäger' badge**

LEFT: Oblt. Siegfried Gottschalt with his Bf 109 D 'Red 5' of 2./ZG 2 at Bernburg shortly before the invasion of Poland. Shortly afterwards this Staffel was redesignated 2./JGr 102. Note the 'Do not step' rectangle on the upper wing flap indicated by a red line. The aircraft carries the Gruppe emblem, the 'Bernburger Jäger' but neither the 2. or 3. Staffel had their own specific marking.

September 1939

"Helmut, leave it to me!"

HELMUT LOHOFF

Lt. Helmut Lohoff of 2./JG 77 later became Staffelkapitän of 7./JG 51 before being captured by Soviet forces on 11 February 1942.

I was born on 31 October 1915. As a youth I began fly gliders and became very excited by this form of transport. I decided to become a pilot and, having finished with my *'Abitur'* and my *'Arbeitsdienst'* (labour service), I enlisted in the army at the *Luftkriegsschulen* Wildpark-Werder and Berlin-Gatow. After a long period of training, I finally reached my goal and was posted as a young *Fähnrich* to IV./JG 132 *'Richthofen'* on 15 August 1938. I was attached to the 12. *Staffel* under command of *Oblt.* Hannes Trautloft. Our *Gruppenkommandeur* was *Hptm.* Janke.

Because our *Gruppe* was always on the move at this time we were nicknamed *'Wanderzirkus Janke'*. For example we transferred to Oschatz on 1 September 1938 in order to be able to cover the Sudeten area should such action become necessary during that crisis. In November 1938, our *Gruppe* was detached from the *'Richthofen' Geschwader* becoming autonomous under the designation I./JG 331. My *Staffel* became 2./JG 331. In May 1939, our *Gruppe* was again redesignated becoming known as I./JG 77.

Late in the afternoon of 4 September 1939, *Lt.* Karl-Gottfried Nordmann and I took off again in a *'schnell Rotte'* (stand-by flight). At about 17.45 hours we spotted a Polish PZL 23 reconnaissance aircraft in the Wielum-Prosna area. The *Rottenführer*, Nordmann, attacked first. He put his aircraft into a high speed dive because the PZL 23 was way below us, but Nordmann's speed was so high that he was unable to get into the right position. To make it worse, the Polish pilot was throwing his aircraft around the sky in all directions. Try as he might, Nordmann was unable to get the enemy aircraft in his 'Revi' sight and passed ahead of him. Then I tried to get into a firing position, but Nordmann cried over the radio:

'Helmut, leave it to me!"

I circled, avoiding our prey, and let Nordmann make a second attack. This time he came in with reduced speed, opened his *'Landeklappen'* (flaps) as well as lowering his landing gear. He only needed one volley of shots and the PZL 23 fell burning from the sky.

This was the first aerial victory made by Nordmann, a future *Eichenlaubträger*, an *'Abschuss'* made in a dangerous manner, at a very slow speed!

ABOVE: A line-up of Bf 109 Es from II./ZG 1 at Przasnisz during the Polish campaign between 11 and 18 September 1939. This unit received the alternative designation JGr 101 from 21 September 1939.

LEFT: A group of pilots from I./JG 21 look quizzically at the two bottles of Schnapps which they used to celebrate at Rostken, in east-Prussia on 17 September 1939, after being awarded the EK II (Iron Cross Second Class) on 17 September 1939 for their operations over Poland. First on the left is Hptm. Martin Mettig (the Kommandeur), in the centre with the bottle is Lt. Gustav Rödel (later awarded the Ritterkreuz with Oak Leaves), with, at right, Lt. Heinz Lange (also to become a Ritterkreuzträger).

Messerschmitt Bf 109 D-1, 3./JG 21, Gutenfeld, East Prussia, September 1939

I./JG 21 had been formed during the summer of 1939 at Jesau as an interim night fighter unit, but was quickly converted to day operations. Its aircraft were unusual in having black-green and yellow striped spinners. I./JG 21 had been formed from I./JG 1 at Jesau and carried a similar badge to the parent unit except that it had a red background. The machine had a splinter pattern of black-green and dark green (RLM 70 and 71) on the uppersurfaces with light blue (RLM 65) underneath.

I./JG 21 (later III./JG 54) badge

ABOVE: Oblt. Georg Schneider, Staffelkapitän of 3./JG 21 in his Bf 109 D-1. He was killed in action on 27 June 1940. The triangular pennant, shows a diving eagle, on the radio mast denotes his rank as Staffelkapitän. I./JG 21 had been formed from I./JG 1 and carried a derivative of the 'Jesau Kreuz' badge but having the white centre cross replaced by the black East Prussian Cross

ABOVE: The Bf 109 D-1s of 3./JG 21 were unusual in having their black-green spinners overpainted with three narrow yellow rings. The unit, which was redesignated 9./JG 54 in July 1940, was based at Gutenfeld in East Prussia for the campaign against Poland.

RIGHT: By 1938, the old method of applying the Swastika on a white disc and red to the tails of its Bf 109s had been superseded by the example shown here. Now the Swastika was simply outlined in white, but the practice of positioning the marking across the fin and rudder was retained. The Bf 109 D-1 in the foreground belongs to 3./JG 21 which was formed in July 1939. The spinner was striped in black-green and yellow.

September 1939

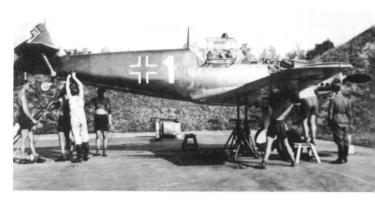

BELOW: Mechanics at work on Lt. Günther Scholz's Bf 109 D. Scholz was the Staffelkapitän of 1./JG 21 (later 7./JG 54) at Gutenfeld in East Prussia.

ABOVE: Taken after returning from his first mission over Poland, this photograph shows the Bf 109 D, 'White 1', piloted by Lt. Günther Scholz, Staffelkapitän of 1./JG 21. At this time the unit was based at Gutenfeld in East Prussia. Note the absence of any unit badges on this aircraft.

Messerschmitt Bf 109 D-1, Lt. Günther Scholz, 1./JG 21 Gutenfeld, September 1939
When Germany invaded Poland in September 1939 several fighter units were still equipped with the Bf 109 D. The pilot of this aircraft, Lt. Günther Scholz, Staffelkaptän of 1./JG 21, later commanded JG 5 based in Norway and Finland. The aircraft was finished in a splinter pattern of black-green and dark green (RLM 70 and 71) with pale blue (RLM 65) underneath.

RIGHT: This Bf 109 D 'Red 13' is undergoing an engine change in a rear factory maintenance hangar. The mechanics appear to be civilians and only rarely were aircraft maintained in such ideal surroundings as most repairs done in the field were carried out in the open irrespective of weather.

LEFT: Lt. Günther Scholz, Staffelkapitän of 1./JG 21 preparing for his first flight over Poland

The telegram read: "Your leave has been cancelled. You are to return to your Gruppe. It is being transferred…"

DIETRICH HRABAK

Dietrich Hrabak served as Gruppenadjutant and Staffelkapitän in 1./JG 138 (later 1./JG 76 and 4./JG 54) before taking command of the Gruppe in August 1940. He was awarded the Ritterkreuz on 21 October 1940 and was appointed Kommodore of JG 52 on 1 November 1942. He was then awarded the Eichenlaubs on 25 November 1943 before leading JG 54 between 1 October 1944 and the spring of 1945. He had a total of 125 victories. He died on 15 September 1995.

I was born on 19 December 1914 and joined the *Reichsmarine* (German Navy) on 8 April 1934. Like several other naval cadets, including the subsequently famous Johannes Steinhoff, I transferred to the *Luftwaffe* as a *Oberfähnrich* on 1 November 1935. Here I received my flying training and, having chosen to become a fighter pilot, was posted to *Jagdgruppe Bernburg* (I./JG 232) on 1 August 1936. On 1 April 1937, I moved again, this time to I./JG 135 (later renamed JG 51) based at Bad Aibling. Here I met my *Kommandeur*, Major Max Ibel and my *Staffelkapitän*, *Hptm.* Hannes Trautloft.

Shortly after the *Anschluss*, on 1 April 1938, I was posted to the new Austrian *Jagdgruppe* at Wien-Aspern (I./JG 138) as *Adjutant*. This *Gruppe* was renamed I./JG 76 on 1 May 1939. Then, on 1 January 1939, I took over the first *Staffel*.

At the beginning of August 1939, I took three weeks holiday and decided, with my friend, the *Gruppen T.O.* to pay a visit to my old comrades at Bad Aibling. The political situation in Europe seemed quiet with no hint of what was to come. We spent the evening at Bad Aibling where we had a good time among our friends. We talked about many things, but no mention was made of the political situation. The day afterwards we drove further into the Alps and had a marvellous time. On 11 August, we paid a visit to a family friend. This person was very agitated, having received a telegram some two days before and was waiting for our arrival with great trepidation. The telegram said: 'Your leave has been cancelled. Return to your *Gruppe* immediately. It is being transferred.' We managed to return to Wien-Aspern that night. In fact the unit was still there, but preparations for moving were well advanced. By 15 August, our ground column was on the road. Two days later, the pilots took off for Stubendorf airfield in Upper Silesia, about 25 km from the Polish-German border.

During the next few days, we did not fly much. We were ordered to keep our field and presence as discrete as possible and also spare our fuel. Nevertheless we came to full alert many times, being ready for take off within five minutes. In the meantime, we anxiously studied the political situation in Europe.

One of our officers was native of Gleiwitz, a city right on the border and only 50 km from our airfield. We thought we might send him to his home town to observe what was happening on the border, but faced with the fuel-restrictions, we constantly postponed the 'mission'. However because the situation did not seem to change and we felt that everything was quietening down, we decided to make the journey in a Kübelwagen on 31 August. The five of us, he, I, the driver and two other officers, all wore civilian clothes. We spent a nice evening at Gleiwitz and decided to return around midnight. Driving back, we were met by endless columns of vehicles and were nearly stopped on the main Gleiwitz-Breslau highway. Something very important was going on and we were miles from our unit!

Despite meeting major difficulties, we finally reached the castle where the officers were billeted, and we could already hear the noise of our Bf 109 engines. I rushed up to my bedroom and discovered a note on my bed which said: 'The attack on Poland is to begin at 04.45 hours. The first *Staffel* of JG 76 is to protect the *Zerstörer* units returning from attack at 05.30 hours in the Rosenberg area.' This left me no time to put on my uniform and I just ran to the airfield as I was. I just had time to don my flying suit, say a few words to my pilots and, at 05.26 hours, we took off for our first war mission.

The weather was bad with low clouds, but on climbing the visibility improved. It was a problem for us to fly in such conditions because we had no instruments and formation flying in bad visibility was also tricky. Nevertheless, we took off and managed to remain together as we climbed through the clouds. When we reached the Rosenberg area, our formation was completely spread out. It took us some time to reform before we could escort the *Zerstörer* (which were also flying Bf 109s). We failed to encounter any enemy aircraft and landed at 06.01 hours, followed by about twelve *Zerstörer*, which were very happy to have finally found a place to land.

No second mission was flown that day. The 2 September was also quiet: only a *'freie Jagd'* being flown without sighting the enemy.

On 3 September we again flew a *'freie Jagd'* mission and encountered a squadron of Polish ground-attack aircraft. During our first attack my engine was hit and I had to belly land in no-mans land. I hid in a wood until I saw German *Panzers* and infantry approaching, after which I was again able to re-join my unit."

September 1939

The next day war began. War with Poland... war with the western armies... war with the world...

HANS VON HAHN

Hans von Hahn was born on 7 August 1914 at Frankfurt/Main. Unfortunately he died of cancer on 5 November 1957, and despite the fact that he was awarded the Ritterkreuz on 9 July 1941, little was known of his career until the following notes were supplied by his family ...

On 1 April 1934, von Hahn joined the *Reichsmarine* at Flensburg-Murwick as a Sea Cadet. In common with many other personnel from this branch of the service, he volunteered for the new *Luftwaffe* in 1935. Following completion of flying training in 1937, he was transferred to the first Gruppe of *Jagdgeschwader* 'Richthofen' at Berlin-Döberitz. At this time the *Gruppe* was commanded by Major Viek. Von Hahn was posted to the third *Staffel* commanded by *Oblt.* Erich von Selle who had trained at Lipezk between 15 April and 15 August 1930. In this *Staffel* he met, among others, the future aces, Walter Oesau and Heinz Bretnütz. While these two went to fight in Spain, von Hahn remained in Germany and was among the men who were detached from I./JG 132 'Richthofen' to create II./JG 334 (later II./JG 53) at Mannheim. He became the *Nachrichten Offizier* (Communications Officer). He now takes up the story: 'In the summer of 1939, I was called by the *Gruppenkommandeur, Major* Hubertus Merhardt von Bernegg, and asked if I wanted to ferry a Heinkel 112 to Romania. I nearly jumped with joy, being so happy and answered: *'Jawohl!'*. I went to the Heinkel factory at Rostock where I found that there were twelve aircraft which had to be ferried to Klausenburg, with their pilots coming from various units from all over Germany. We were given brief instruction on the aircraft which was new to us and began our journey. Firstly we flew to Dresden, then to Vienna and finally Zagreb in Yugoslavia. We were dressed as civilians when we left Germany. When we landed in Zagreb, the Yugoslavian pilots welcomed us to their airfield, later inviting us to a very nice evening at Agram. 'Heavy' wine and Slivowitz seemed to flow in limitless quantities and we soon realised that they were trying to find out about our operational status. We politely told them that we were only Heinkel factory pilots and were not able to give any military information. Nevertheless, it was a very cordial get–together. The next morning we took off for Belgrade, and flew on from there to Klausenburg.

'Here we received a hearty welcome. The Romanian officers were real comrades and showed us everything we wanted to see. It was clear that, from a political point of view, they were pro-German. They complained about their regime and finally declared that if we had one day to fight against each other, this would be against their wishes and only to do their duty. We handed over our aircraft to them and, after a memorable day, went to Bucharest by train. On our arrival, a Romanian officer took us to our splendid hotel, then gave us a tour of the city which impressed me tremendously with its beautiful buildings and areas. Unfortunately, our time was too short and we were soon back at the civilian airfield from where we flew in a Lockheed to Budapest. From there, a Junkers brought us to Berlin and we finally returned to Rostock for the debriefing. When we arrived at Rostock, things had changed a lot. The station was full of soldiers, and many areas were guarded. When we asked why, it was explained that mobilisation was under way. At any moment the war could start against Poland and that would also mean a war with France and England. Hearing this we hurriedly returned to the airfield in the hope of going back to our units as soon as possible. A comrade took me with him to our unit and we flew, full of hope, to Mannheim to prepare for war. We arrived just in time. The next day war began. War with Poland, war with the western armies, war with the world.

'Our first task was to guard the Rhine, the *'Wacht am Rhein'* as it was known. While our colleagues conquered Poland in a few days, we only performed survey flights against the French and didn't even cross the border... '

LEFT: The Bf 109 D to the left of this photo, marked with a double chevron, belonged to Hptm. Hans Gentzen, the Kommandeur of JGr 102. This photo was probably taken at Gross Stein airfield towards the end of the war against Poland. He was awarded the EK I (Iron Cross First Class) for this success and, at the age of 34, was probably the first ace of the Second World War. He was killed in a take off accident on 22 May 1940 by which time his Gruppe had been re-equipped with the Bf 110. Note that the variations of camouflage on the Bf 109s and other aircraft in the photo. Note the mixture of camouflage finishes. The Bf 109s in the foreground have light blue (RLM 65) fuselage sides whereas the one behind has a splinter pattern of black-green and dark green (RLM 70 and 71).

September 1939

RIGHT: A Bf 109 E coded 'White 5' operated by 1./JG 1 which had been formed at Jesau in East Prussia from 1./JG 131 by way of 1./JG 130. The badge was the arms of the city of Jesau.

ABOVE: Bf 109 E-1s from I./JG 1 being prepared for a mission against Poland in early September 1939. For the campaign, the Gruppe was moved from its original base of Jesau to Allenstein, also in east Prussia.

ABOVE: Three officers from I./JG 1 discuss an operation against Poland early in September 1939 at Mühlen airfield. Note the 'Jesau Kreuz' insignia carried by the cockpit of the Bf 109 E and the inertia starting handle. The spinner was painted in red and black-green with a narrow white ring in the centre with the aircraft camouflaged in a splinter pattern of black-green and dark green (RLM 70 and 71) on the uppersurfaces with light blue (RLM 65) underneath.

ABOVE: Exhaust fumes engulf a Bf 109 E of I./JG 1 starting up. Oblt. Wilhelm Balthasar (left) looks on as the aircraft prepare for a mission against Poland probably at Allenstein in East Prussia early in September 1939. These Bf 109 Es have black-green and white spinners and finished in (RLM 70 and 71) splinter pattern.

RIGHT: Bf 109 Es of I./JG 1 (later III./JG 27) were based in East Prussia and operated out of the same airfield as the Hs 123 ground attack aircraft of LG 2 shown in the background. The Bf 109s probably offered some escort protection for the Hs 123s. The aircraft also has a black-green and white spinner but has the latter finish of having pale blue (RLM 65) on the fuselage sides. Note the cowling in the foreground showing the top part of a white two figure number, possibly 13, 15 or 17.

September 1939

A bad result for our first mission of the war!

HEINZ LANGE

Lt. Heinz Lange of I./JG 21 survived the war, becoming an ace with 70 'kills' (including one in the west and 24 Il-2 bombers). He would end the war as Kommodore of JG 51 and a holder of the Ritterkreuz.

I was born in Köln on 2 October 1917. I had intended to join the army in December 1936, hoping to become an officer, but when the opportunity came to transfer to the *Luftwaffe*, I volunteered, my father having been a pilot during the First World War. Up to this time I had not flown. Because the *Luftwaffe* was still being established, our training was quite leisurely at this time. Eventually I completed about 150 flying hours from the beginning of my training until I became a qualified fighter pilot.

On 15 July 1939, *Hptm*. Martin Mettig, a former marine officer of the *Reichswehr* who had volunteered to join the *Luftwaffe* early on, was asked to establish I./JG 21. The new *Gruppe* received many technicians from an existing unit, *Major* Bernhard Woldenga's I./JG 1. Some of the pilots such as Günther Scholz and Joachim Wandel, had already gained operational fighter experience in Spain. For them, as for me who had transferred from JG 26, the equipment at I./JG 21 was a throw back to the past. We had flown the Bf 109 E but at JG 21, we had to take over old '*Doras*'. Our *Gruppe* (the only one in the *Geschwader*) was based at Gutenfeld in East-Prussia, with the task of protecting Königsberg from potential bombing attacks.

The war against Poland began on 1 September 1939. Our main job was to escort *Luftwaffe* bombers, principally He 111s, in the Varsovia area. At 14.36 hours, our *Gruppe* of around 30 aircraft, transferred to Rostken which was to be our operational airfield. Our mechanics transferred in a few Ju 52s.

At 16.16 hours, we took off on our first combat sortie of the war. We had to escort a bomber group to its target in the vicinity of Varsovia. As we rendezvoused with the bombers, the weather was so bad that the gunners failed to identify us as friends and opened fire. As this was only their first or second mission they were quite nervous. Our *Kommandeur, Hptm*. Martin Mettig, tried to fire a recognition cartridge but unfortunately, his pistol was not fixed properly, and it went off inside the cockpit. The resulting fire ball burned his hands, feet and thighs. He then jettisoned his canopy (with the fixed antenna mast) in an attempt to clear the smoke. But now with no radio, he could not inform us of his intention to return to base. Because of this, half our pilots followed him, me amongst them. We landed without problems. Meanwhile, the other part of the Gruppe became involved in an air battle with Polish PZL 24s. Four of them were claimed shot down, but six of our pilots had to make emergency landings and were captured. The other pilots lost their way as the visibility was poor. They also made emergency landings, but this time inside our lines. A bad result for our first war mission!

Our *Gruppe* flew against Poland until the end of the campaign, and then we took a short rest at Jesau in East-Prussia. At the beginning of October, we were sent to Plantlünne in western Germany to patrol the Dutch border. At that time, we didn't have much to do, calling the period the '*Sitzkrieg*' or 'sitting war'. Occasionally we scrambled our aircraft, and once, on 30 October 1939, I intercepted a twin-engined aeroplane which I could not recognise. At first I thought it might be German, perhaps a He 111. We were flying at an altitude of 300-500 meters (1,000 to 1,600 feet) between white clouds. It was nice weather. Then the tail gunner began to fire at my *Katschmarek* and I. This confirmed to me that it was an enemy aircraft, so I returned fire. I hit him and he crashed. I was upset to see that no-one escaped from aircraft. It is perhaps strange to imagine now that we were happy to see our adversaries bail out safely. The action took place over Germany because, at that time, it was strictly forbidden to cross the Dutch border.

On 1 February 1940, our *Kommandeur, Hptm*. Mettig was transferred to the *Stab* of JG 54 to become its first *Kommodore*. The new *Kommandeur* of I./JG 21 became *Hptm*. Fritz Ultsch.

From left to right Hptm. Franz-Heinz Lange, Lt. Max-Hellmuth Ostermann both later awarded with the Ritterkreuz and Oblt. Friedrich Behrens (missing in action on 12 December 1940). Ostermann also received the Eichenlaub mit Schwertern zum Ritterkreuz des Eisernen Kreuz. He was killed in action on 9 August 1942 near Amossovo in Russia.

LEFT: A Bf 109 E-1, coded 'Red 7' of 2./JG 1, taxies out for a sortie over Poland with a number of Bf 110s in the background. The aircraft carries the black, white and yellow 'Jesau Kreuz' badge of I./JG 1.

LEFT: Hptm. Hannes Trautloft, (standing with hands on hips) with the men of 2./JG 77 during the Polish campaign. The Bf 109 E in the background 'Red 1' was painted black-green (RLM 70) on the uppersurfaces with light blue (RLM 65) underneath. The aircraft also has a red circle outlined in white and three white fuselage bands. The one nearest the front appears to be double the width of the other two. These markings may have been used as identity markings during training and manoeuvres. The gun ports have also been painted yellow, not an uncommon practice, as was the spinner.

I./JG 77 Badge
'Wanderzirkus Janke'
(Janke's Wandering Circus)

ABOVE: A group of pilots from 2./JG 77 play cards and chat in front of one of the Staffel's Bf 109s early in the campaign against Poland. 'Red 13', W.Nr.3378, was normally piloted by Oblt. Ekkehard Priebe who had served with 1.J/88 in Spain before becoming Milch's Adjutant for a short period. He held this position until September 1939 but, following the Polish campaign, he became Staffelkapitän of 2./JG 77. He claimed one victory on 11 October 1939.

LEFT: Close up of the nose of a 3.(J)/LG 2 Bf 109 E-3 coded 'Brown' (or possibly Red) '15' piloted by Heinz 'Pietsch' Bretnütz. The name 'Peter' was painted in white on the engine cowling. 'Peter' was a common nick-name which Bretnütz also carried on his Bf 109 in Spain in which he claimed three victories. He was later awarded the Ritterkreuz on 22 October 1940.

RIGHT: The same Bf 109 E-3 of .(J)/LG 2 as above preparing for a mission against Poland early in September 1939. Around this time several third Staffeln (including 3./JG 26 and 3./JG 51 in addition to 3.(J)/LG 2) began to replace their highly conspicuous yellow numbers with brown.

September 1939

ABOVE: Georg Seelmann of 2./JG 77 cuddles his dog with his Bf 109 E, coded 'Red (or Brown) 14', in the background. Seelmann was awarded the Ritterkreuz in October 1941.

ABOVE: The Zylinderhut (top hat) Staffel emblem attached to the radio mast in the foreground, right was probably introduced at 2.(J)LG 2 by Hptm. Joachim Schlichting, a pilot with 2.J/88 who had scored five victories in Spain. The emblem continued to appear until the end of 1944, on Bf 109s of 2./JG 77 later designated 2.(J)/LG 2.

ABOVE: Details of the Red and White shield carried by Oblt. Erwin Bacsila as his personal emblem on his Bf 109 E whilst he was with II./ZG 1's (JGr 101). The shield is the coat of arms of the city of Vienna (Wien), the city where he studied.

Messerschmitt Bf 109 E-1 of Oblt. Erwin Bacsila, Adjutant of II./ZG 1 (JGr 101)

Fürstenwalde, September 1939. This aircraft is pictured on 19 September, the day the city of Danzig fell to German forces. Two days later, the Gruppe was temporarily redesignated JGr 101. The Bf 109 had overall black-green (RLM 70) uppersurfaces with pale blue RLM 65) beneath. The single chevron denoting the aircraft of the Gruppenadjutant was painted on the fuselage side together with the horizontal bar of the second Gruppe.

ABOVE: A view showing the other side of Bacsila's aircraft.

LEFT: Oblt. Erwin Bacsila, the Gruppenadjutant of II./ZG 1 poses with his Bf 109 E-1 on 19 September 1939 at Danzig, the day on which German forces took the city. Two days later, II./ZG 1 was temporarily redesignated JGr 101 before being re-equipped with the Bf 110 during the spring of 1940. Note the aircraft also has yellow gun troughs.

September 1939

BELOW: The PZL P-23 'Karas' two-seat reconnaissance aircraft was the one of the most common types in service with the Polish Air Force. This aircraft is shown after suffering a crash landing.

ABOVE: German soldiers inspect a damaged PZL 11c fighter. The Polish Airforce was no match for the Luftwaffe and was mostly destroyed on the ground in the first few days of the war.

BELOW LEFT AND RIGHT: The German destruction of Poland had been swift and total, exactly 21 days. The Polish forces were no match for the new mechanised warfare the Germans unleashed upon them. What the German forces had not yet taken, the Russians were quick to grab as their share of the spoils. Warsaw had been heavily bombed causing huge amounts of damage. Some valiant Polish troops tried to hold out as long as possible but the full and total surrender was inevitable. The surviving Polish army defending Warsaw finally surrendered to the Germans without any terms and conditions. These two photos show the surrender took place on a bus without any ceremony, the Polish commanders surrendering the 100,000 surviving Polish soldiers as prisoners of war.

Development and Tactics

During 1939 the *leichte Jagd* (or 'light' fighter) force was re-equipped with the Messerschmitt Bf 109 E single–engined fighter, although several units flew the earlier models, and a few still had Arado Ar 68s. Powered by a 1,175 hp Daimler-Benz DB 601 A engine which gave it a maximum speed in the order of 550 km/h (340 mph), the *Emil* or E-series Bf 109 was one of the finest fighters in the world at the time. The only aircraft in Europe that could meet it on equal terms was the Supermarine Spitfire which was just entering service with the Royal Air Force. Even this excellent fighter lacked the Bf 109's direct fuel injection and three-blade variable pitch propeller at this time.

By the outbreak of war, two variants of the Bf 109 E were in service, the E-1 and E-3. The E-1 carried an armament of four 7.9 mm MG 17 machine-guns, two in the wings and two above the engine firing through the propeller. The E-3 had the wing machine-guns replaced by two 20 mm MG FF cannon which considerably improved the fighter's fire power. Although an excellent aircraft, the Bf 109 did have some faults including poor visibility, particularly on take-off, and its narrow track outwards retracting undercarriage rendered it rather unstable while taxying.

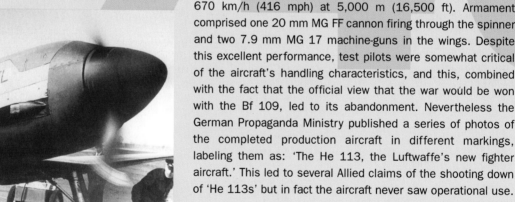

Apart from the Bf 109, two new single-engine fighters were also flying in Germany by June 1939, one of which was to see operational service, one of which was not. The He 100 was designed by the Heinkel company to cure many of the faults exhibited by the He 112. The aircraft's structure was radically simplified, an inward retracting wide track undercarriage was fitted and surface evaporation cooling was to be adopted. The prototype made its first flight on 22 January 1938, eight further test aircraft following. One of these, the specially modified He 100 V8, broke the world speed record on 30 March 1939 with a speed of 746.59 km/h (463.92 mph).

In spite of this success, the surface evaporation cooling system proved impossible to perfect and was replaced by a conventional semi-retractable radiator in the proposed production model, the He 100 D. Three D-0s and twelve D-1s were eventually completed, the variant attaining a maximum speed of 670 km/h (416 mph) at 5,000 m (16,500 ft). Armament comprised one 20 mm MG FF cannon firing through the spinner and two 7.9 mm MG 17 machine-guns in the wings. Despite this excellent performance, test pilots were somewhat critical of the aircraft's handling characteristics, and this, combined with the fact that the official view that the war would be won with the Bf 109, led to its abandonment. Nevertheless the German Propaganda Ministry published a series of photos of the completed production aircraft in different markings, labeling them as: 'The He 113, the Luftwaffe's new fighter aircraft.' This led to several Allied claims of the shooting down of 'He 113s' but in fact the aircraft never saw operational use.

BELOW: Heinkel test pilot Hans Dieterle sat in the cockpit of the He 100 V8 before breaking the world speed record.
BOTTOM: Hans Dieterle runs up the engine while mechanics make the final checks before take–off.

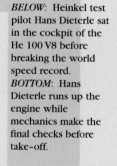

ABOVE: The He 100 V8 during the world record breaking flight

LEFT: Heinkel staff congratulate Hans Dieterle after he had broken the world speed record on 30 March 1939 in the He 100 V8. This aircraft was fitted with a specially-boosted DB 601 engine which allowed it to attain a speed of 746.59 km/h (463.92 mph). Shortly afterwards the record was broken by the Messerschmitt Me 209, this record standing, for piston-engined aircraft for over thirty years.

RIGHT: Two mechanics pose with a He 100 D experimental fighter which still carries its factory code and paintwork before the aircraft was re-painted in spurious markings. Powered by a 1,175 hp Daimler-Benz DB 601 Aa engine, the aircraft had an impressive performance, but test pilots were critical of its handling characteristics.

BELOW AND BELOW RIGHT: These German propaganda photos were intended to fool the Allies into thinking this aircraft was fully operational by showing line-ups and labeling them as 'He 113s'. Although potentially an excellent fighter, the He 100 D-1 (to give the aircraft its proper designation) never entered service with the Luftwaffe. All He 100 were painted black green (RLM 70) and dark-green (RLM 71) on the uppersurfaces and light-blue (RLM 65) underneath. These photos clearly show the existence of a splinter pattern.

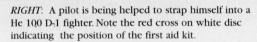

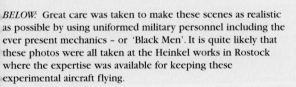

RIGHT: A pilot is being helped to strap himself into a He 100 D-1 fighter. Note the red cross on white disc indicating the position of the first aid kit.

BELOW: Great care was taken to make these scenes as realistic as possible by using uniformed military personnel including the ever present mechanics – or 'Black Men'. It is quite likely that these photos were all taken at the Heinkel works in Rostock where the expertise was available for keeping these experimental aircraft flying.

LEFT: In an attempt to convince the Allies into thinking the He 100 had entered service with the Luftwaffe the twelve completed He 100 D-1s were painted in standard fighter camouflage with added spurious identification numbers and markings. Many photos of the type were published in German war time publications.

He 100 D-1 carrying spurious operational markings

The twelve He 100 D-1s completed were finished in black–green (RLM 70) and dark green (RLM 71) uppersurfaces and pale–blue (RLM 65) underneath. These aircraft were photographed at varying times sporting one of three different emblems, a white 'lightning flash', a 'dagger piercing a hat' and a 'moon smoking a pipe'.

ABOVE: A He 100 D-1 makes a low-flying pass over the camera showing off its distinctive cranked wing shape. The aircraft was extremely small having a wingspan of only 9.4 metres (30 ft 10 inches) and a length of 8.18 metres (26 ft 10 inches inches).

RIGHT: Another propaganda photo of the line-up of 'operational He 113s'. This photo clearly shows existence of a splinter pattern. This is a contemporary hand coloured photo showing a reasonable facsimile of how these aircraft might have appeared.

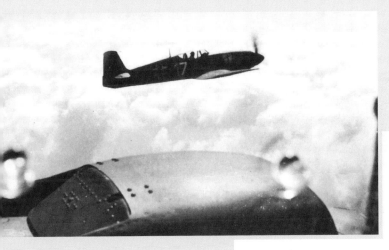

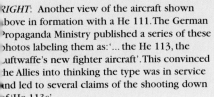

LEFT: Photographed from a He 111, this photo shows 'White 17' another He 100 D-1 with spurious operational markings designed to fool Allied intelligence into thinking the type had entered service with the Luftwaffe. The emblem on the nose is a 'dagger piercing a hat'.

RIGHT: Another view of the aircraft shown above in formation with a He 111. The German Propaganda Ministry published a series of these photos labeling them as: '... the He 113, the Luftwaffe's new fighter aircraft'. This convinced the Allies into thinking the type was in service and led to several claims of the shooting down of 'He 113s'.

'Dagger piercing a hat' badge

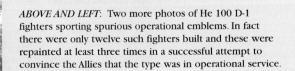

ABOVE AND LEFT: Two more photos of He 100 D-1 fighters sporting spurious operational emblems. In fact there were only twelve such fighters built and these were repainted at least three times in a successful attempt to convince the Allies that the type was in operational service.

As part of the programme to convince Allied intelligence that the He 100 was in service with the Luftwaffe some aircraft were photographed at night, in an attempt to suggest that the type was also intended to be used as a night fighter. For this series of photos, a badge was applied to the aircraft consisting of a 'moon smoking a pipe'. Careful study of the photos show evidence of new fuselage paintwork around the badge area .

'Moon smoking a pipe ' badge

A new fighter

Although the He 100 was abandoned, the RLM did ask Focke–Wulf to develop a new fighter to supplement the Bf 109 during the spring of 1938. Designated Fw 190, the new aircraft was entirely conventional in layout, but differed from Germany's earlier fighters in being powered by a BMW 139 fourteen–cylinder radial engine. The Soviet Rata fighter, several examples of which had been captured in Spain, had demonstrated the usefulness of such a rugged fighter powered by this type of engine. In addition, the Focke-Wulf design team under Kurt Tank, had seen that other nations, particularly the USA, were pushing ahead with the design and development of high–powered radial engines for fighters and they had no wish to lag behind.

The prototype of the new fighter, the Fw 190 V1, made its first flight on 1 June 1939 piloted by Focke-Wulf's chief test pilot, *Flugkapitän* Hans Sander. It was powered by a 1,500 hp BMW 139 engine which was closely cowled, its line continuing forward to blend into a special ducted spinner which it was anticipated would further reduce drag. Although offering little air resistance, this ducted spinner proved impractical and was removed at an early stage. Even then the engine suffered constant overheating problems and it was not until late July 1941 that the fighter entered service with the *Luftwaffe*. As will be seen as the story of the *Jagdwaffe* unfolds, the fighter was to become one of the finest of the war, but not before suffering constant teething troubles.

ABOVE: On 1 June 1939, the first prototype of the new fighter the Fw 190 V1 was rolled out at the Focke-Wulf factory in Bremen. Here the machine is scrutinised by one of the senior technicians as Flugkapitän Hans Sander, Focke-Wulf's chief test pilot runs up the engine in readiness for the first flight.

In the year that proceeded the outbreak of war, aircraft production in Germany failed to expand, and by the autumn of 1939 the position was only just beginning to improve towards the figure of 700 aircraft per month. Due to a difficulty in obtaining skilled workers, many younger men being needed for the armed forces, production failed to expand beyond 800 aircraft per month during the first year of the war. At the outbreak of war the *Luftwaffe* had a strength of about one and half million men, almost two-thirds of these in the anti-aircraft arm. Of the remaining third, only about 15 per cent were aircrew.

LEFT: After making a successful first flight, Hans Sander brings the machine in to land on a grass strip at the Focke-Wulf Bremen factory. The aircraft was powered by a 1,500 hp BMW 139 engine which was closely cowled with a novel new ducted spinner which was hoped would reduce drag. However, this subsequently proved impractical and was only ever fitted to the Fw 190 V1 and V2 prototypes.

Tactics

Apart from possessing a superb fighter in the Bf 109, the *Jagdwaffe* also had the advantage of having a cadre of pilots who had gained valued combat experience in Spain. One of the tactics learned in this theatre was the development of a new combat formation, this later proving invaluable during the Second World War. Given the high closing speeds of modern fighter aircraft, it became vital to spot the enemy first and to protect vulnerable tail areas. Eighty per cent of all aerial kills are attained with the aircraft shot down never knowing the enemy is there, and the attack usually comes from the rear. In the traditional formation of three aircraft tightly grouped together (known in Germany as the *Kette*) the pilot of the high-speed fighter had far too much of his attention taken in avoiding collision with his wingmen, leaving him vulnerable to attack from the rear.

To overcome this problem, the quiet and brilliant fighter pilot, Werner Mölders, came up with the idea of having aircraft flying in loose pairs (the *Rotte*). Each *Rotte* was capable of acting as an independent formation in search, defence or attack, but could co-operate with another pair (the combination being known as a *Schwarm*) to increase firepower and overall visual protection. The fighters were spread some 200 m (650 ft) apart which permitted the pilots to concentrate on finding the enemy rather than straining to fly in parade ground formation. Each aircraft of the *Schwarm* took positions resembling the fingers of an outstretched hand viewed from above - often known as the Finger Four' in the Royal Air Force. The leader of each group of two (the *Rottenführer*) visually searched the forward hemisphere while his wingman (the *Rottenflieger* or *Katschmarek*) covered the rear.

In defence, if one *Rotte* was attacked, the distance between it and the other *Rotte* of the *Schwarm* permitted the second section to turn in towards the enemy and open fire. In an offensive operation, the *Rottenführer* would lead the attack while his wingman concentrated in covering his rear. During the aerial battles against the Spitfires and Hurricanes of the RAF that developed in 1940, the British still used the tight formation of three aircraft which rendered them at a severe disadvantage to the free-ranging German formations. The lesson was learned quickly however, and soon the RAF, and later the USAAF, adopted the same tactics. The tactic is used to this day, although the distance between aircraft has increased to thousands of metres/feet.

The 'Sitzkrieg'

SEPTEMBER 1939 TO FEBRUARY 1940

BELOW: The wreckage of an RAF Bristol Blenheim from No.107 Squadron being examined by German personnel. Of the four aircraft from the squadron that were dispatched against German Naval ships on 4 September 1939, only one returned.

Inevitably, the invasion of Poland had resulted in Britain and France declaring war on Germany on 3 September 1939. Sadly for the Poles, the Western Allies were unable to give any direct support. Following the successful conclusion of the campaign, Hitler made another peace offer to Britain and France on 5 October 1939. This was instantly rejected. Four days later, the *Führer* angrily issued *OKW Direcktive Nr.6* which affirmed his intention of striking westward as soon as possible. *Direcktive Nr.7,* issued thirteen days later, called for active reconnaissance flights to be made across the French border, these to be escorted by *Luftwaffe* fighters where necessary. The Directive also allowed for the attacking of the Royal Navy at their British bases.

On 19 October, Generals Halder and von Brauchitsch presented a preliminary plan for an attack on the west. Entitled *'Fall Gelb'* ('Contingency Yellow'), the plan was revised ten days later. It was to use a total of 102 divisions of which nine were armoured and six motorised to destroy Allied forces north of the Somme and gain possession of Dunkirk and Boulogne. With this aim in mind, Bock's *Heeresgruppe B* was specially strengthened to 43 divisions and was to attack west of Luxembourg on both sides of Liége. At the same time, von Rundstedt's *Heeresgruppe A* would attack further south. Initially, it was proposed that only a small part of The Netherlands around Maastricht would be crossed by the *6.Armee* on its westward drive, but following Göring's objection that the remaining part of Holland might be used as bases by RAF bombers, it was decided to invade the whole of that country.

Just after the war with Poland began, the first clash took place between RAF bombers and *Luftwaffe* fighters. During the first weeks of hostilities both sides had undertaken not to bomb enemy territory, attacks being confined to warships and supply vessels. The first of these came on 4 September 1939, the day after Britain had declared war on Germany. Ten RAF Blenheims from Nos.107 and 110 Squadrons bombed the pocket battleship *Admiral Scheer* in the Schillig roads near Wilhelmshaven, hitting the warship with three bombs, but all failed to explode. One Blenheim crashed on the forecastle of the cruiser *Emden* when hit by heavy flak. Another 19 RAF Wellingtons from Nos.9 and 149 Squadrons attacked the battleships *Scharnhorst* and *Gneisenau* at Brunsbüttel of which seven were lost. Five were shot down by flak and two were intercepted by the Bf 109s of II./JG 77 based at Nordholz. Despite the poor prevailing weather conditions for single-engined fighters, two *Luftwaffe* pilots, Fw. Alfred Held and Fw. Hans Troitzsch, pressed home their attacks and managed to shoot down the Wellingtons, both from No.9 Squadron. These were the first RAF aircraft to be destroyed by the *Luftwaffe*.

Four days later the first fighter versus fighter action took place when a *Schwarm* of Bf 109 Es from I./JG 53 clashed with six Curtiss Hawk 75s of the French *Groupe de Chasse* II/4 over the Saarland. The French claimed two Bf 109s shot down, one of which was the aircraft piloted by the *Staffelkapitän* of 1./JG 53, *Oblt*. Werner Mölders, who force-landed with a damaged engine. That evening a second action took place when *Lt*. Paul Gutbrod from JG 52 shot down a Potez 637 reconnaissance aircraft near Karlsruhe. This was the first French aircraft to be destroyed by the *Jagdwaffe* and the first victory claimed by JG 52.

On 9 September, *Ofw*. Walter Grimmling of 1./JG 53 flying 'White 8' shot down a twin-engined enemy bomber at 11.25 hours north-east of Saarbrücken at 5,900 m. This was the first confirmed victory claimed by JG 53. Next day 2./JG 53 under *Oblt*. Rolf Pingel flew a number of combat operations in the Saarbrücken area from around 13.30 hours. A Mureaux 115 from *Groupe* I/520 was shot down about an hour later by *Uffz*. Heinrich Bezner and Lt. Claus. Grimmling and Bezner were later awarded the Iron Cross Second Class (EK II).

On 16 September a number of fighter units were transferred to the Western Front from Poland because they were now needed more on that front. The units included I.(J)/LG 2 and I./JG 77. Three days later JG 53 lost its first pilot killed when *Uffz*. Dill of 3./JG 53 crashed to his death at 11.15 hours - the reason remains unknown. On the same day the second *Gruppe* of JG 53 claimed its first victory, a French Potez shot down by a Bf 109 E of 4./JG 53 piloted by *Oblt*. Schulze-Blanck.

BELOW: Oblt. Werner Mölders shortly before being shot down, is seen here still wearing his Spanish flying jacket. He has the distinction of being one of the first Luftwaffe pilots to be shot down in the West. He force landed and was able to continue with operations.

ABOVE: Uffz. Alfred Held of II./JG 77 is congratulated for shooting down the first British bomber of the Second World War.

September–December 1939

ABOVE: The Fairy Battle was no match for the Bf 109 E and the RAF squadrons received severe losses which soon rendered the type withdrawn from combat.

By this time, the British Advanced Air Striking Force had reported itself ready for operations in France. On 20 September this force clashed with the *Luftwaffe* for the first time when three Fairy Battles from No.88 Squadron were bounced by a *Schwarm* of Bf 109s while on a photo-reconnaissance patrol. The Battle's vulnerability to fighter attack was immediately obvious when two were shot down. However, the third aircraft managed to escape, its gunner, Sgt. F. Letchford, managing to shoot down one of the attackers. Four days later the first Bf 109 E to fall into Allied hands, 'Black 9' of 2./JG 71, landed at Rimling near Sarreguemines in the Moselle Department of France. The aircraft was evaluated by both French and British test pilots.

The week beginning Monday, 25 September 1939, was to prove very successful for the *Jagdwaffe*, II./JG 77, JGr 152 and *Stab,* I. and II./JG 53 shooting down eleven Allied reconnaissance aircraft with a twelfth making a forced landing. On the 27 September, for example, three Fairy Battles of No.103 Squadron RAF were intercepted by French Curtiss Hawks. The Battles immediately fired off recognition signals and descended to ground level. The French realised their mistake and flew off but almost immediately three Bf 109s attacked. At least one Battle was shot down, but one of the British aircraft *may* have shot down a Bf 109. Next day *Fw.* Klaus Faber, claimed I./JG 1's first victory, a Blenheim, but the best day for the Germans came on the 30th. Just after midday, 2./JG 53 claimed five Fairy Battles from No.150 Squadron RAF. In fact one of the Battles did return to base but was damaged beyond repair. Following this, the type was withdrawn from unescorted daylight operations. Later in the day, I./JG 53 clashed with French fighters, the *3.Staffel* shooting down two Moranes and a Curtiss Hawk. The action was by no mean one sided however, the *Gruppe* losing four Bf 109s. A fifth aircraft, piloted by *Uffz.* Rudolf Schmidt of 5./JG 53 was also lost and another damaged in a crash landing. During September, the French Air Force claimed a total of 27 victories in the west.

ABOVE: Early evidence of RAF losses sustained at the hands of the *Jagdwaffe* is shown here with the remains of shot down aircraft. The aircraft in the foreground is a Fairly Battle.

BELOW: On 12 November 1939 Major Carl Schumacher, previously Kommandeur of II./JG 77, was promoted to Oberstleutnant and made Kommodore of the newly created Stab of JG 1. His command included II./JG 77, II.(J)/186, JGr 101 and 10.(N)/JG 26. Here Schumacher, second from the right, studies a map of the German Bight area probably at his headquarters at Jever airfield.

On 1 October two new German fighter *Gruppen* were formed, I./JG 27 under *Hptm.* Helmut Riegel and III./JG 53 under *Hptm.* Werner Mölders. Five days later a third *Gruppe,* II./JG 51, was formed by renaming the old I./JG 71 under *Hptm.* Günther Matthes. Apart from the establishment of new units, the *Jagdwaffe* also developed a method of improving its defence against Allied aircraft intruding into German air space by co-operating closely with its observer network directing interceptions by radio. The first success with this method came on 6 October when *Lt.* Berthel of 2./JG 52 shot down a French LeO 451 bomber.

At the beginning of October, to prepare for 'Fall Gelb', the *Luftwaffe* was regrouped, with the *Fliegerdivisionen* being redesignated *Fliegerkorps*. Von Richthofen's command was designated *VIII.Fliegerkorps* on the 5th and the fighter force had I.(J)/LG 2 transferred from the east to *Luftflotte 2* and I./JG 77 and JGr 102 to *Luftflotte 3*. On the 18 October *VIII.Fliegerkorps* moved its headquarters to Koblenz by which time it had 46 *Staffeln* including I.(J)/LG 2 and the whole of JG 53. Within a week Richthofen's forces had been further bolstered by the arrival of I./JG 77, the commencement date for 'Fall Gelb' being announced by Hitler as Sunday, 12 November. At the end of October, JG 27, JG 52 and JGr 126 had been transferred to Richthofen's command, but various command, weather and logistical problems were to delay the offensive .

On 22 November, the second Bf 109 E to fall intact into Allied hands was captured when an aircraft of 1./JG 76 landed by mistake at Woerth in the Bas-Rhin Department of France due to fog.

Meanwhile, conscious of the threat to the German fleet by RAF bombers, *Luftwaffe* fighter forces in the Heligoland Bight had been re-organised on 12 November. *Major* Carl Schumacher, *Kommandeur* of II./JG 77, had been promoted to *Obstlt.* and given control of the newly created *Stab* of JG 1. His command included II./JG 77 (now under *Major* Harry von Bülow), II.(J)/186 under *Hptm.* Heinrich Seeliger, JGr 101 under *Major* Reichardt and 10.(N)/JG 26 under *Oblt.* Johannes Steinhoff.

September–December 1939

ABOVE: One of the first types of RAF aircraft to be destroyed by Luftwaffe fighters was the Wellington bomber. During the attack by Nos.9 and 149 Squadrons carried out on 4 September 1939 against German Naval ships, two of these aircraft, from the former unit, were shot down by II./JG 77.

The first test for the reorganised force came on 3 December when 24 Wellington bombers from Nos.38, 115 and 149 Squadrons attacked two cruisers near Heligoland. The Wellingtons were shot at by anti-aircraft defences and intercepted by fighters, but one of the latter was promptly claimed shot down by a gunner from No.38 Squadron. The British forces suffered no losses. Encouraged by this success, twelve Wellingtons from No.99 Squadron attacked the cruisers *Nürnberg* and *Leipzig* in the outer Jade anchorage eleven days later. This time they were repelled by heavy flak and attacks by II./JG 77, the British losing five Wellingtons destroyed with a sixth crashing during the return flight to England.

If 14 December had proved disappointing for the RAF, 18 December was to be disasterous. Around 10.00 hours, twenty-four Wellingtons from Nos.9, 37 and 149 Squadrons took off from East Anglia to fly an armed reconnaissance of the Schillig Roads and Wilhelmshaven. Two aircraft soon returned to base with problems, but the remaining twenty-two were spotted by *Freya* radar at about 13.50 hours. First to attack were six Bf 109s of 10.(N)/JG 26, but they were soon joined by the other fighter and destroyer squadrons, the battle ranging far out to sea. Having studied the previous operations, the fighters attacked from the side or from above rather than from astern. This meant that the Wellingtons could not use their powerful nose and tail gun turrets against the fighters and, with no armour or self-sealing fuel tanks, they suffered dreadfully from the fighters gunfire. In total ten were shot down, two more crashed into the sea during the return and three others were written off on landing. Worst hit was No.37 Squadron which lost five of its six aircraft.

The RAF had thought, as had the *Luftwaffe*, that bombers could operate successfully in daylight, defending themselves by the concentrated fire from their gun turrets, but this was not the case. As JG 1 later reported: *'The British seem to regard a tightly closed formation as the best method of defence, but the greater speed of our Bf 109s and Bf 110s enabled them to select their position of attack."* Their report concluded: *'It was criminal folly on the part of the enemy to fly at 4,000 to 5,000 m in a cloudless sky with perfect visibility. After such losses it is assumed that the enemy will not give the Geschwader any more opportunities of practice shooting at Wellingtons."*

The success of Schumacher's fighter command led to the establishment of three similar commands known as *Jagdfliegerführer* on 1 January 1940. *Jafü 1* was Schumacher's old command, *Jafü 2*, with its headquarters at Dortmund was established under *Gen.Maj.* Kurt von Döring and *Jafü 3* at Wiesbaden was led by *Gen.Maj.* Hans Klein. On the same day two more fighter *Gruppen* were formed, II./JG 27 under *Hptm.* Erich von Selle and III./JG 3 under *Hptm.* Walter Kienitz. Just previously, a second *Gruppe* had been added to JG 3 under *Hptm.* Erich von Selle.

On 27 December, 'Fall Gelb' was rescheduled to take begin sometime between 9 and 14 January but a disaster befell on 10 January. *Major* Helmut Reinberger, liaison office between *Fliegerführer 220* and *Luftflotte 2* was offered a lift in a Bf 108 by *Major* Erich Hönmanns, commander of Loddenheide airfield, to fly him to Köln airfield. On the way to Köln, Hönmanns got lost and was forced to land at Maasmechelen in Belgium. Although it was strictly against regulations, Reinberger was carrying the order of operations for *Luftflotte 2*, and these, although partly burnt, were captured. The documents partly revealed the plan for the invasion to the Allies, and it was again postponed. The commander of *Luftflotte 2*, Hellmuth Felmy, was held responsible for the disaster and cashiered, his place taken by Albert Kesselring. In turn, Hans-Jürgen Stumpff took over *Luftflotte 1*. On 18 February a revised 'Fall Gelb' plan was proposed in which the roles undertaken by Bock and von Rundstedt were reversed.

Meanwhile air operations continued on the Western Front, those by the bombers being rendered impotent by political restraint. Nevertheless the *Jagdwaffe* took a steady toll of Allied reconnaissance aircraft including the French Bloch MB 131 and Potez 637 and the British Blenheim IV. Particularly successful were the Bf 109s of JG 53, II./JG 77 and JGr 152. Experience was to show that in fighter versus fighter combat, the French MS 406, Bloch 152 and Curtiss Hawk 75 and the British Hawker Hurricane while better than the Bf 109 D, were all inferior to the Bf 109 E. The only French fighter capable of meeting the E-series on anything like equal terms was the Dewoitine D.520 but, up until May 1940, the only unit to be equipped with the type was GC I/3 and this was based at Cannes for operational development.

September–December 1939

Expansion of the Luftwaffe's Fighter Units – 1 May 1939 to 10 May 1940

1 May 1939	15 July 1939	1 January 1940	10 May 1940
I.(J)/LG 2	I.(J)/LG 2	I.(J)/LG 2	I.(J)/LG 2
I./JG 1	I./JG 1	I./JG 1	I./JG 1
I./JG 2	I./JG 2	I./JG 2	I./JG 2
		II./JG 2 [1]	II./JG 2
			III./JG 2 [2]
	10.(N)/JG 72 [3]	11.(N)/JG 2	IV(N)./JG 2 [4]
I./JG 3	I./JG 3	I./JG 3	I./JG 3
		II./JG 3 [5]	II./JG 3
		III./JG 3 [6]	III./JG 3
	I./JG 20 [7]	I./JG 20	I./JG 20
	I./JG 21 [8]	I./JG 21	I./JG 21
I./JG 26	I./JG 26	I./JG 26	I./JG 26
II./JG 26	II./JG 26	II./JG 26	II./JG 26
		III./JG 26 [9]	III./JG 26
		I./JG 27 [10]	I./JG 27
		II./JG 27 [11]	II./JG 27
I./JG 51	I./JG 51	I./JG 51	I./JG 51
	I./JG 71 [12]	II./JG 51 [13]	II./JG 51
I./JG 52	I./JG 52	I./JG 52	I./JG 52
	11./JG 72 [14]	II./JG 52 [15]	II./JG 52
			III./JG 52 [16]
I./JG 53	I./JG 53	I./JG 53	I./JG 53
II./JG 53	II./JG 53	II./JG 53	II./JG 53
		III./JG 53 [17]	III./JG 53
	I./JG 70 [18]	I./JG 54 [19]	I./JG 54
I./JG 76	I./JG 76	I./JG 76	I./JG 76
I./JG 77	I./JG 77	I./JG 77	I./JG 77
II./JG 77	II./JG 77	II./JG 77	II./JG 77
6.(J)/186	6.(J)/186	II.(J)/186	II.(J)/186

Notes:

(1) II./JG 2 was formed on 15 December 1939.

(2) III./JG 2 was formed on 27 April 1940.

(3) 10.(N)/JG 72 was officially formed on 15 July 1939 from a basis provided by II./JG 53.

(4) 10.(N)/JG 72 became 11.(N)/JG 2, a 10.(N)/JG 2 having been newly formed late in 1939. The newly formed 10.(N)/JG 26 then became 12.(N)/JG 2, the three Staffeln then becoming IV.(N)/JG 2. This unit eventually became III./NJG 1.

(5) II./JG 3 was formed in late 1939.

(6) III./JG 3 was formed on 1 January 1940.

(7) I./JG 20 was officially formed on 15 July 1939 at Döberitz from a basis provided by I./JG 2.

(8) I./JG 21 was officially formed on 15 July 1939 at Jesau from a basis provided by I./JG 1.

(9) III./JG 26 was formed on 23 September 1939 from other parts of JG 26 and II./ZG 26.

(10) I./JG 27 was formed on 1 October 1939.

(11) II./JG 27 was formed on 1 January 1940.

(12) I./JG 71 was officially formed on 15 July 1939 from a basis provided by I./JG 51 and I./JG 52.

(13) I./JG 71 was redesignated II./JG 51 on 6 October 1939.

(14) 11./JG 72 was officially formed on 15 July 1939.

(15) II./JG 52 was probably formed from a nucleus provided by 11./JG 72 and possibly 1./JG 71 in September 1939.

(16) III./JG 52 was formed in April 1940.

(17) III./JG 53 was formed on 1 October 1939.

(18) I./JG 70 was formed on 15 July 1939, from a basis provided by I./JG 51.

(19) I./JG 54 was formed from I./JG 70 on 15 September 1939.

ABOVE: A line up of Bf 109 Ds. During the Polish campaign many Luftwaffe units were being rapidly re-equipped with the latest variant, the Bf 109 E, but the 'Doras' were still being used although they were progressively transferred to other units for a secondary role and training.

ABOVE: A line-up of Bf 109 Es from 1. and 2./JG 53 photographed at Wiesbaden-Erbenheim airfield at readiness to defend Germany's western borders in September 1939.

ABOVE: Mechanics at work on the Daimler-Benz DB 601 A engine of a Bf 109 E-3. The aircraft carries a segmented upper surface camouflage pattern of black-green (RLM 70) dark green (RLM 71), standard for the early months of the Second World War, with pale-blue (RLM 65) underneath.

September–December 1939

ABOVE: Close-up showing the night owl 'Pik As' badge of 10.(N)/JG 72 on an Ar 68 F-1.

Badge of 10.(N)/JG 72

ABOVE: An Arado 68 F-1, probably seen at Oedheim/Heilbronn in September 1939. The machine was fitted with flame dampers for nocturnal operations.

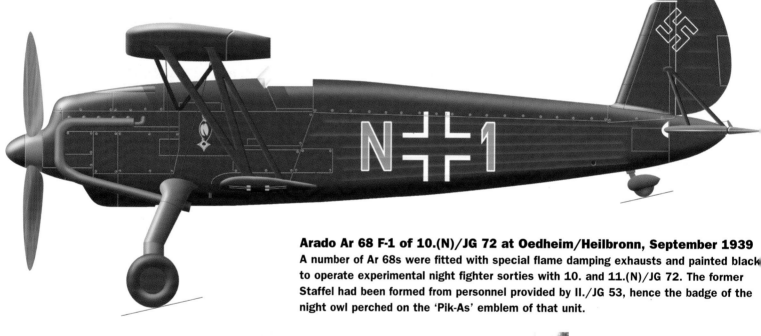

Arado Ar 68 F-1 of 10.(N)/JG 72 at Oedheim/Heilbronn, September 1939
A number of Ar 68s were fitted with special flame damping exhausts and painted black to operate experimental night fighter sorties with 10. and 11.(N)/JG 72. The former Staffel had been formed from personnel provided by II./JG 53, hence the badge of the night owl perched on the 'Pik-As' emblem of that unit.

LEFT: Even the Luftwaffe had to perform drill wearing the 'Stahlhelm'. Here the ground crew have been put through their paces at Mannheim-Sandhofen airfield in September/October 1939. Note the Bf 109 Es from 3./JG 53 in the background whose duties were to patrol over the Franco-German border.

September–December 1939

RIGHT: A mechanic removes the chocks from under the wheels of a Bf 109 E of 3./JG 53 as it prepares for a border patrol flight in September/October 1939. This aircraft has conventional dark green and black-green uppersurfaces with light-blue beneath, although JG 53 tested a large variety of camouflage schemes using various shades of greys and greens.

**Personal emblem on a
Bf 109 E belonging to JG 53**

BELOW: Ofw. Walter Grimmling (left) is congratulated for the destruction of the Geschwader's first enemy aircraft on 9 September 1939. He was flying the aircraft in the background, coded 'White 8' at the time of the victory.

ABOVE: A mechanic completes the painting of a personal emblem on this Bf 109 E probably belonging to 1. or 2./JG 53 at Wiesbaden-Erbenheim during September 1939.

RIGHT: Oblt. Wilhelm Balthasar of 1./JG 1 at the Dummersee (near Osnabrück) on 23 September 1939 after having just received the Iron Cross Second Class (EK II) which can be seen attached to his tunic button. This was in addition to the decorations he had been awarded in Spain (where he scored seven victories). Note the small metallic Staffelkapitän pennant on the radio mast of the Bf 109 in the background. White numbers were used to identify the first Staffel.

LEFT: Uffz. Ernst Schulz of 3./JG 1 relaxes against his Bf 109 E-3, coded 'Yellow 6' at Vörden airfield on 26 September 1939. The yellow rings around the black-green spinner also indicate that the aircraft belonged to the third Staffel. Schulz was taken prisoner on 18 September 1940 following combat with RAF fighters. He suffered severe injuries and died on 12 December.

September–December 1939

LEFT: A line-up of Bf 109 Es of I./JG 2 at Berlin-Döberitz airfield, September 1939. At this time only one Gruppe of the 'Richthofen Geschwader' existed; II./JG 2 being added on 15 December 1939 and III./JG 2 on 27 April 1940.

BELOW: Taken at Berlin-Döberitz airfield during the beginning of September 1939, this photo shows Fw. Franz Jänisch (centre) of I./JG 2 who served previously in Spain. Jänisch was Mölders's wingman in Spain where he achieved one victory.

LEFT: Lt. Hans-Kurt Graf von Sponeck of JG 2 sat in the cockpit of his Bf 109 D holding his pet Scottish terrier. Besides the JG 2 'Richthofen Geschwader' badge, his aircraft had a caricature of his dog painted below the cockpit.

BELOW: An unidentified pilot on horseback in front of 3./JG 2's Bf 109 Es, coded 'Yellow 3', at Berlin-Döberitz airfield in early September 1939. On the Messerschmitt's engine-cowling can be seen the blue flag with the name 'Horrido!' which the Staffelkapitän, Hptm. Hennig Strümpell, brought from Pomerania. This badge was later to be associated with Helmut Wick.

**Personal Emblem of
Lt. Hans Kurt Graf von Sponeck JG 2**

September–December 1939

LEFT: Members of 3./JG 3 relax at Brandis in East Germany with a Bf 109 E, coded 'Yellow 11' in September 1939. This Staffel operated in the defence of the Reich under Luftgau-kommando IV headquartered in Dresden, while Staffeln were involved in Poland. Note the wooden maintenance tool box for Bf 109 E, W.Nr. 3202. Note also how 'BF' has been abbreviated with two capital letters which was against the normal convention of 'Bf'.

BELOW: Taken at Merseburg in September 1939, this photo shows the Bf 109 E flown by Oblt. Hans 'Assi' Hahn, an experienced fighter instructor from 1935, who was later to take over 4./JG 2. The aircraft carries his personal cockerel insignia, 'Hahn' being the German word for cock. This aircraft also appears to have yellow gun troughs.

Personal emblem of Oblt. Hans 'Assi' Hahn

LEFT: Luftwaffe 'Black Men' (mechanics) at work on a Bf 109 E of Stab I./JG 20, possibly the aircraft piloted by Lt. Otto Kath. The aircraft was photographed in September 1939 and it is interesting to note that even at this stage, the unit carried the wavy line marking which identified a third Gruppe however I./JG 20 was not redesignated III./JG 51 until July 1940.

Messerschmitt Bf 109 E-1 of 1./JG 20, Brandenburg-Briest, September 1939

JG 20, like many other fighter units of the time, had a splinter pattern of black-green (RLM 70) and dark green (RLM 71) on the uppersurfaces with pale blue (RLM 65) beneath. The camouflage patterns varied considerably and it was quite difficult to see the dividing line between the two colours. The badge of 1./JG 20, a white bow and arrow, was retained when the Staffel was redesignated 7./JG 51 in July 1940.

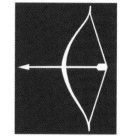

Badge of 1./JG 20 later redesignated 7./JG 51

BELOW: Lt. Harald Jung of 1./JG 20 (later 7./JG 51) with one of his Staffel's Bf 109 Es at Brandenburg-Briest in mid September 1939.

LEFT: Although I./JG 20 was formed on 15 July 1939 and was not redesignated III./JG 51 until 4 July 1940. Despite this, the unit's aircraft had the third Gruppe wavy line marking painted on its aircraft as early as September 1939. For the operations against Poland, I./JG 20 was based at Sprotau in Silesia, moving to Brandenburg-Briest on 9 September for the defence of Berlin. This photo shows Bf 109 Es of 1./JG 20 with white numbers.

ABOVE: Four pilots from 1./JG 20 in conversation at Brandenburg-Briest in September 1939. From left to right are: Lt. Hermann Staiger (later awarded the Ritterkreuz), Lt. Gottfried Schlizter (killed in combat on 6 August 1942 after claiming 25 victories), unknown and Oblt. Walter Oesau (Staffelkapitän of 1./JG 20 who was also later awarded the Ritterkreuz, Oaks Leaves and Swords but was later also killed in action on 11 May 1944).

LEFT: A Rotte of Bf 109s of I./JG 20 roar off overhead while mechanics prepare other aircraft for take off. Note that the unit, which did not become III./JG 51 until July 1940, still carries the 'wavy line' marking of that I./JG 20.

ABOVE: Oblt. Walter Oesau, Staffelkapitän of 1./JG 20 standing in front of a Bf 109 E-1 at Brandenburg-Briest in September 1940. 1./JG 20 became 7./JG 51 in 1940 retaining their original emblems. The aircraft carries the splinter pattern of black-green (RLM 70 and 71) on the uppersurfaces with light-blue (RLM 65) underneath.

Emblem of 2./JG 20

ABOVE AND LEFT A pilot from 2./JG 20 climbs into the cockpit of Bf 109 E coded 'Red 7' at Brandenburg-Briest. The 'black cat' badge used by the second Staffel was similar to the 'red cat' badge of 4./JG 52. These two photos were used in many wartime German propaganda publications.

September–December 1939

LEFT: 8./JG 26 used the popular cartoon character 'Adamson' as its Staffel emblem, seen here on a Bf 109 E coded 'Red 11'. This unit had been formed on 23 September 1939 from 4./JG 26, the Staffelkapitän being Oblt. Eduard Neumann.

BELOW: Apart from carrying emblems on their aircraft, units also painted these on their vehicles. This photo shows the 'Adamson' cartoon character painted on one of JG 26's staff cars.

Personal emblems of Hptm. Karl Ebbighausen

BELOW: When the original 'Adamsonstaffel', 4./JG 26 was redesignated 8./JG 26 on 23 September 1939, a new 4./JG 26 was formed under Hptm. Karl Ebbighausen. His Bf 109 E carried the script 'S' badge of JG 26 painted below the cockpit together with two personal emblems. Ebbighausen was had also served with the Legion Condor (hence the use of the 'Mickey Mouse'), first with 3.J/88 and then with the Stab.

**JG 26 'Schlageter'
Geschwader Badge**

Messerschmitt Bf 109 E-3 flown by Uffz. Stefan Litjens of 4./JG 53, late autumn 1939
During the 'Sitzkrieg' JG 53 flew regular patrols along the Franco-German border, some of its Bf 109s carrying most unusual camouflage schemes. The fuselage of this aircraft had irregular patches of pale–blue (RLM 65), RLM grey (RLM 02) and dark green (RLM 71) applied to both sides of the fuselage and wing uppersurfaces.

JG 53 (Pik As) Geschwader

BELOW: Hptm. Erich Mix poses in front of his Bf 109 E at Wiesbaden-Erbenheim in September 1939. At this time JG 53 began to experiment with a variety of camouflage schemes using a splinter pattern combination of dark-green (RLM 71) RLM grey (RLM 02) and light blue RLM 65).

ABOVE: What appears to be the same aircraft as in the photo below only by this time the new national style markings had been applied. The 'White 5' numeral and horizontal bar appear the same but the Balkenkreuz appears to be freshly painted. It is probable that the Hakenkreuz is also in the new position on the fin only.

RIGHT: Patrolling the border in the area of Bad Bergzabern–Pirmasens these Bf 109 E-3s of 4./JG 53 are flying in close formation. The nearest aircraft, W.Nr.1244, 'White 5' was piloted by Uffz. Stefan Litjens. II./JG 53 operated out of Mannheim–Sandhofen during the winter of 1939-1940.

BELOW: Typical of the 'Sitzkrieg' period are these Bf 109 Es of Stab I./JG 53 at Wiesbaden-Erbenheim in September 1939. At this time most fighter operations were confined to patrolling the Franco-German border and escorting Luftwaffe reconnaissance aircraft over France.

September–December 1939

LEFT: Lt. Hartmann Grasser of JGr 152 was awarded the EK 2 for shooting down a French Curtiss Hawk 75 fighter on 24 September 1939. His wingman, Lt. Horst Elstermann, also shot down a Hawk 75 on the same day. Both German aircraft were hit during the action and force landed, being 30 and 40% damaged respectively. Hartmann Grasser survived the war as Kommodore of JG 210, a Geschwader composed of Soviet fighter pilots from the Wlassow army. With a tally of 103 victories, he was awarded the Ritterkreuz with Eichenlaubs.

ABOVE: Hptm. Karl-Heinz Lessmann, Kommandeur of JGr 152 photographed on the same day as Lt. Hartmann Grasser after having been awarded the EK 2 (Iron Cross Second Class) for shooting down the Bloch MB 200 bomber, No 163, piloted by Cdt. Delozammen, commander of GB II/31, during the afternoon of 9 September 1939. This action took place in the Zweibrücken area. Around this time the Bf 109 Ds were rapidly being replaced by the newer Bf 109 E variant. The obsolete aircraft were then relegated to secondary roles.

LEFT CENTRE AND LEFT: Hptm. Karl-Heinz Lessmann's Bf 109 D photographed at Illesheim or Biblis. This variant was often known by the German phonetic alphabet letter for 'D' – 'Dora'. This Bf 109 variant was rapidly being replaced with the 'E' – 'Emil' at this time .

September–December 1939

Messerschmitt Bf 109 E-3 flown by Oblt Kurt Sochatzy, 3./JG 76, October 1939 at Rhein-Main

It was not unusual for German fighters of this period to have their uppersurfaces painted black-green (RLM 70) overall with pale blue (RLM 65) underneath.

I./JG 76 (later II/JG 54)

ABOVE, RIGHT AND BELOW: An Austrian pilot with 3./JG 76, Oblt. Kurt Sochatzy poses in front of his Bf 109 E coded 'Yellow 8' at Rhein-Main airfield in October 1939. Sochatzy served in Spain for a short time before returning to his Gruppe. He participated in the invasion of Poland and shortly afterwards was promoted to Oberleutnant. He was awarded the Ritterkreuz on 12 August 1941 nine days after having baled out over Kiev and taken prisoner by the Russians.

September–December 1939

LEFT: The spinner of this Bf 109 E from 2./JG 1 had a black-green (RLM 70) nose with a narrow white ring and red hub. The propeller wes also painted black-green and had the VDM logo on the front of each blade.

BELOW: I./JG 1 took part in the operations against Poland before being transferred to Vörden airfield for border patrol duties. This aircraft, belonging to 2./JG 1, carried a 'Red 6' outlined in white.

Messerschmitt Bf 109 E-1 of 2./JG 1, Vörden, October 1939

After operating for a short time in Poland, I./JG 1 was transferred to north-west Germany to guard the border against incursions by French and British aircraft. Their aircraft carried black–green (RLM 70) and dark green (RLM 71) splinter pattern on the uppersurfaces with light blue (RLM 65) underneath. The 'Jesau Kreuz' badge was the arms of the town where the unit had been formed.

RIGHT: A pilot from 2./JG 1 is helped with his parachute prior to an operation from Vörden airfield in October 1939.

BELOW: Rather unusually, this Bf 109 E of 1./JG 1 carries the early style Balkenkreuz but with the Hakenkreuz painted on the fin only. Normally, this was painted across both fin and rudder when matched with the early style cross. The aircraft made a belly landing at Vörden airfield in October 1939.

September–December 1939

LEFT: A mechanic from I./JG 1 starting the engine of a Bf 109 E at Vörden, in October 1939. Judging by the cleanliness of this machine it appears to have just been delivered. Note the yellow gun troughs which were a common feature on many Bf 109s but no doubt these would have quickly stained after firing.

BELOW: Uffz. Emil Clade of 1./JG 1 sat in the cockpit of his Bf 109 E coded 'White 2' at Vörden airfield around October 1939. The code 'White 2' was used by Clade for some months. At this time, the Jagdwaffe were still using white to identify the first Staffel in a Gruppe, red for the second and yellow for the third.

BELOW: Oblt. Hans 'Assi' Hahn, who had just been posted to JG 2, at Schafstädt, with a number of Bf 109 Es in the background. The unit had been moved from Berlin-Döberitz just after the outbreak of the Second World War, this photo being taken in October or the beginning of November 1939.

BELOW: A typical muddy scene taken late in October or early November 1939 just after JG 2 had transferred to this temporary airfield at Schafstädt.

An unknown emblem – possibly from a Staffel in the second Gruppe of JG 2

LEFT: A personal emblem painted on the nose of this Bf 109 E of JG 2 (possibly the second Gruppe) photographed at Schafstädt airfield in October or the beginning of November 1939.

LEFT: Just after take off, a Bf 109 E of 3./JG 52 retracts its undercarriage

ABOVE: Oblt. Helmut Kühle, Staffelkapitän of 3./JG 52 addresses his men at Bonn-Hangelar airfield in October 1939. Kühle had served with J/88 from 3 February 1937 before transferring to I./JG 234. He was killed as Major and Gruppenkommandeur of III./JG 6 during the well-known and murderous 'Operation Bodenplatte' on 1 January 1945.

LEFT: The Lt. and Technical Officer of I./JG 52 (sitting on the wing of this Bf 109 E) talks to a group of 'black men' (mechanics) at Bonn-Hangelar airfield, October 1939.

BELOW: A 3./JG 52 Bf 109 E, coded 'Yellow 1', begins its take off run from Bonn-Hangelar airfield in October 1939. This airfield was used by I./JG 52 from 28 September to 15 November 1939.

September–December 1939

BELOW AND RIGHT: A series of photographs of the Bf 109 E, 'Yellow 2' piloted by Lt. Dietrich Wickop of 3./JG 52 at Bonn/Hangelar during August/September 1939. Note that the aircraft still carries the early style Balkenkreuz with narrow white outline and the Swastika painted across fin and rudder.

Detail of octane triangle
Yellow (RLM 04) outlined in white

Bf 109 E-1 flown by Lt. Dietrich Wickop, 3./JG 52, August 1939
This aircraft had overall black–green (RLM 70) uppersurfaces with a yellow (RLM 04) number '2'. At this time, I./JG 52 was based at Bonn-Hangelar and later took part in border protection duties.

BELOW: An excellent view of the yellow '87' octane triangle edged in white which marked the main fuel filler point for the Bf 109 E.

ABOVE: Detail of the starboard side of 'Yellow 2'. Note the electrical connection socket in the centre of the '2'.

September–December 1939

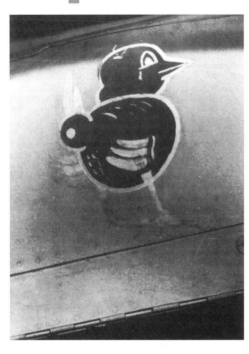

RIGHT: Lt. Dietrich Wickop of 3./JG 52 poses in front of his Bf 109 E, 'Yellow 15' at Bonn-Hangelar airfield in October 1939. This was, in fact, Wickop's first aircraft.

LEFT: A close up detail of 2./JG 21's 'Sparrow' badge depicted on the nose of a Bf 109 E. The badge appears always to be painted with the bird looking to the right irrespective on which side of the aircraft it was painted.

BELOW: Photographed after crash landing somewhere on the Western Front in October 1939, this Bf 109 E of 2./JG 21 had its individual number 'Red 14' painted in an unusual position, but not uncommon for this Gruppe. 2./JG 21 was redesignated 8./JG 54 in July 1940. Note the Staffel emblem on the engine cowling which was later adopted by 8./JG 54 'Grünherz' (Green Heart).

Badge of 2./JG 21, later adopted by 8./JG 54 when the unit was redesignated

Messerschmitt Bf 109 E-3 of 2./JG 21, north-west Germany, late October 1939

This aircraft carried an unusual combination of national markings and camouflage. The uppersurfaces of the fuselage and wings were painted in a splinter pattern of RLM grey (RLM 02) and dark green (RLM 71) with the fuselage sides light blue (RLM 65). The aircraft carried the early style Balkenkreuz but the Hakenkreuz was painted, in the new position on the fin only. Another unusual feature was the painting of the identification number below the cockpit.

September–December 1939

RIGHT: Lt. Dietrich Wickop of 3./JG 52 (third from the left) photographed with other members of his Schwarm. At this time, October-November 1939, 3./JG 52 was based at Bonn/Hangelar. This Bf 109 E-3 carries the new style Balkenkreuz but unusually for this early period, also has had what appears to be RLM Grey (RLM 02) mottle applied over the whole of the uppersurfaces and fuselage sides. As most Messerschmitt aircraft left the factory painted in light-blue (RLM 65) this aircraft may have been delivered in this finish to the unit who then applied the mottling and at the same time the new style crosses and Hakenkreuz.

Messerschmitt Bf 109 E-1, W.Nr. 878 flown by Uffz. Hermann Neuhoff of 7./JG 53, October 1939
The aircraft was painted black-green (RLM 70) on the uppersurfaces and light blue (RLM 65) underneath. An unusual feature was the small 'Red 2' positioned in the centre of the chevron.

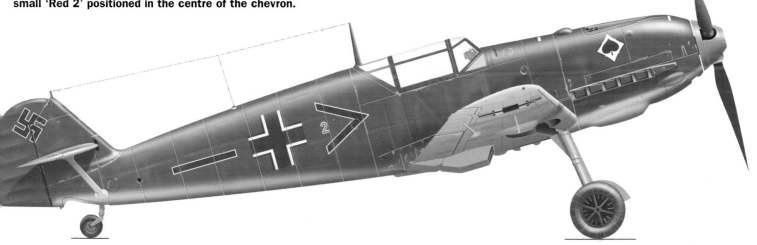

LEFT AND BELOW' Two views of Uffz. Hermann Neuhoff's Bf 109 E-1, W.Nr 878 as indicated on the cockpit and nose covering, of 7./JG 53. The III. Gruppe of JG 53 was formed in October 1939 under Hptm. Werner Mölders, the most successful german fighter pilot in the Spanish Civil War. Aircraft of JG 53 adopted the 'Pik-As' (Ace of Spades) badge around this time, which was used by the unit up to the end if the Second World War.

JG 53 'Pik As' Geschwader badge

September–December 1939

ABOVE, BELOW AND BELOW LEFT: This crashed Bf 109 E, 'White 14' of 1./JG 26 (the staffel badge can be just be seen under the cock[pit], was temporarily repainted with French blue, white and red national insignia before being transported across Germany in an attempt to mislead German civilians into thinking that only Allied aircraft were being shot down.

1./JG 26 badge

RIGHT: An unusual view looking at the business end of a Bf 109 E. The off-set of the MG 17 guns are clearly visible and it would appear this aircraft has just received some brand new nose panels and engine cowling, as the whole nose section is painted light blue (RLM 65), which was a common colour used by Messerschmitt when newly completed Bf 109s left the factory. Note the cockpit canopy framing was black-green (RLM 70).

September–December 1939

We flew our first combat mission, the first involving the 'Richthofen Geschwader' since the end of the First World War...

HENNIG STRÜMPELL

Following the end of the Spanish Civil War, I returned to Berlin where I had to write a lot of reports. Udet, Stumpff and others were very interested to read details of our activities in Spain. Then I asked to return to my 'old' *Geschwader* (JG 2) at Döberitz and took over the third *Staffel* which was still equipped with He 51s. My *Kommodore* was *Oberst* von Massow and the first *Gruppenkommandeur* was *Major* Carl Viek.

Having tested and flown the Bf 109 in Spain, I was not happy until we were finally re-equipped with this fantastic aircraft. At first we received a few *'Bertas'* and then the *'Doras'* followed. This aircraft, new to most of my pilots, was quite difficult to fly, its narrow track undercarriage being responsible for several crashes. We had a lot of losses before the war, more than much later after the war with the famous but difficult F-104 Starfighter.

During the invasion of Poland, our *Gruppe* was posted to the east of Berlin in order to protect the capital but, in reality, we did not think that this crisis would result in a major war.

In October 1939, *Hptm.* Jürgen Roth became our new *Kommandeur* then, on 2 November 1939, our *Gruppe* moved to Frankfurt/Rebstock with about 40 aircraft. Our main task was to protect our borders, France and the United Kingdom having declared war after our invasion of Poland. We flew patrols at altitudes of between 6 and 7,000 metres and *'Freie Jagd'* between 3 and 4,000 metres, often working with JG 53. The area was divided into two sections: one for the *Richthofen Geschwader*, the other for the *Pik-As*. Our third *'Staffel'* mess was housed in a wooden barracks which was very cold during the bad winter weather. The airfield itself posed problems because it was too short for the Bf 109. Nevertheless we were very busy during this time, trying to fly daily patrols towards the west. We were often given permission to enter enemy territory up to 50 kilometres (30 miles). Normally we had no fear of the French anti-aircraft guns, finding enemy fighters much more dangerous.

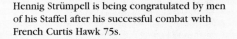

Hennig Strümpell is being congratulated by men of his Staffel after his successful combat with French Curtis Hawk 75s.

On 22 November 1939, we flew our first combat mission, the first involving the *Richthofen Geschwader* since the end of the First World War. My *Staffel* was involved and two of our pilots, *Leutnant* Helmut Wick and *Oberfeldwebel* Erwin Kley were victorious. I recently found their stories. Wick, who was later to become the *Luftwaffe's* top-scoring pilot, reported:

On 22 November, two Schwärme from our third Staffel flew a border protection patrol. Suddenly we were attacked by 14 enemy aircraft from out of the sun, all Curtiss Hawk 75s. I had four of them coming at me from behind. Nevertheless none of them scored hits on me, and after a few evasive manoeuvres, I was able to get the last French aircraft in my sights, firing a short burst which hit him and caused him to crash. I only fired a few rounds.

His comrade, Ofw. Erwin Kley gave more details:

My Schwarm was attacked from out of the sun. Having avoided their first pass, we managed to gain altitude, but were attacked again, once more from out of the sun. I had two Curtiss Hawks trying to shoot me down. Then I managed to manoeuvre towards them, getting one in my sights. I fired and the aircraft immediately went into a dive: I think I hit the pilot. The other French aircraft then attacked me with renewed vigour and the fighting became more intense, an enormous dog fight with everyone shooting and manoeuvring. During this, I saw a Curtiss chasing one of my comrades and I turned in order to put myself behind him. I opened fire and hit him, only stopping firing when he hit the ground. So I was able to claim two victories on my first combat mission.

Author's note: On that day, 3./JG 2 was in the air at about 11.30 hours, its task being to act as cover for two reconnaissance Dorniers, when they met the Curtiss H-75s of GC II/4 in the Phalsbourg area, some 55km (35 miles) south of Saarbrücken. Lt. Wick's victim was probably Adj. Camille Plubeau who managed to crash land his aircraft (No 169) although wounded. Kley was initially credited with two kills, but this was later reduced to one, that being the aircraft (No 95) piloted by Sgt. Saillard who was killed. His first claim was not confirmed. Both German pilots received the EK II (Iron Cross Second Class). This account is especially important in that it warns readers that claims were not always accepted or realistic.

Wick was killed on 28 November 1940 as Kommodore of JG 2 and Stbfw. Erwin Kley was shot down and killed by a Spitfire during the air fighting over Dieppe on 19 August 1942. Strümpell himself took over command of I./JG 2 on 20 June 1940.

September–December 1939

Messerschmitt Bf 109 E-1 of 3./JG 27, Münster-Handorf, November 1939
I./JG 27 was formed on 1 October 1939 under Hptm. Helmut Riegel, after receiving a batch of
Bf 109 E-1s. The unit's aircraft carried the standard splinter camouflage pattern of black–green
(RLM 70) and dark green (RLM 71) uppersurfaces with pale blue (RLM 65) underneath.

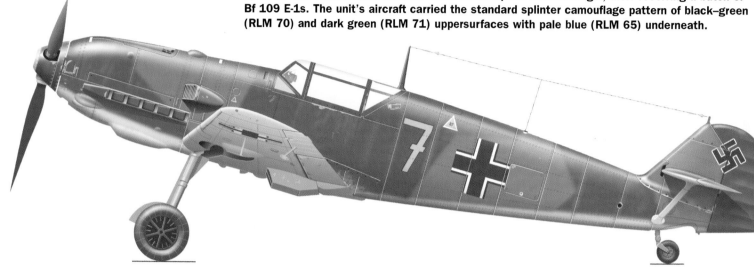

2./JG 1 badge

ABOVE: This Bf 109 E, marked with a typically Germanic 'Yellow
7', belonged to 3./JG 27 based at Münster-Handorf in November
1939. Note the distinctive white angle marking painted on top of
the landing flaps. I./JG 27 was established at Münster on 1
October 1939 under Hptm. Helmut Riegel. The Adjutant was Oblt.
Gerhard Homuth who had been posted from I.(J)/LG 2 where he
had flown with the Kommandeur Trübenbach's Kunstflugstaffel
(aerobatic squadron).

ABOVE: A Bf 109 E from 2./JG 1 undergoing weapons calibration at Vörden. For
this, the aircraft was propped up on trestles and firing of the machine-guns
practiced against a special target.

LEFT: A Bf 109 E from I./JG 1 taxies out to its take-off point after heavy rain at
Vörden airfield in November 1939. Note that this aircraft, like several others of
the period, had very large Balkenkreuz national insignia above the wings.

September–December 1939

**1./JG 21 (later 7./JG 54)
'winged clog' badge variant as shown below**

ABOVE: A line-up of camouflaged Bf 109s of 1./JG 21 photographed at Plantlünne airfield at the beginning of November 1939. After operating in Poland I./JG 21 moved to Plantlünne, near the Dutch-German border.

ABOVE: This Bf 109 of 1./JG 21 carries the black and white winged clog badge painted on both sides of the engine cowling. This emblem was retained by 7./JG 54 after 1./JG 21 received this new designation in July 1940.

ABOVE: This close-up gives excellent detail of the cockpit area of the early Bf 109 E. The mechanic seated in the cockpit is technician Philipp Schmelzer of 2./JGr 101 who later became a pilot with JG 26. This aircraft is dedicated to 'Die Erika', no doubt the name of the pilot's female involvement. The small white inscription reading 'GhdPidn–asmes' is a mystery.

RIGHT: Mechanics at work on a Bf 109 E-1 of I./JG 51 at Mannheim-Sandhofen. This unit was formed from I./JG 135 by way of I./JG 233

September–December 1939

LEFT: A Bf 109 E of 9./JG 26 comes in to land at Essen-Mulheim in November 1939.

BELOW: Both Hans-Joachim Müncheberg (left) and Gerhard Strasen (right) were first class athletes, particularly the latter who would probably have pursued international careers if the Second World War had not intervened. Just like Gotthard Handrick (who won the Pentathlon Gold Medal at the 1936 Olympic Games), they were assigned to JG 26. Müncheberg claimed a total of 135 victories before being killed, and Strasen, a very experienced fighter pilot, ended the war as Gruppenkommandeur of III./JG 4.

ABOVE: Joachim Müncheberg, Gruppenadjutant of III./JG 26 photographed in November 1939. On 7 November, Müncheberg intercepted the Blenheim (serial number L1325) of No.57 Squadron R.A.F. piloted by Plt. Off. H. R. Bewley, and shot it down into the Rhine near Opladen. This was the second victory claimed by JG 26 and the first of what was to become Müncheberg's total of 135. All the British crew bailed out safely but were taken prisoner.

RIGHT: Early in the war, two symbols were used to identify aircraft of the third Gruppe of a fighter Geschwader. Some units had a wavy line painted behind the fuselage cross while others, like III./JG 26 shown here, use a vertical bar.

September–December 1939

LEFT: Uffz. Artur Beese of 9./JG 26 poses in front of his Bf 109 E, coded 'Yellow 11' at Essen-Mühlheim, around November 1939. Beese was killed in combat on 6 February 1944. Note the large crosses on the top of the wings.

RIGHT: Major Ernst von Berg standing in front of his aircraft marked with the double chevron of a Gruppenkommandeur. This photo was probably taken on 1 November 1939 at Essen-Mühlheim when von Berg took over command of the newly formed III./JG 26. He was to be killed in action in 1943.

LEFT: A group of officers from the Gruppenstab of III./JG 26 pose in front of a Bf 109 E at Essen-Mühlheim on 1 November 1939 just after the unit was formed. From left to right are: Lt. Peter Göring, Oblt. Walter Horten (one of the famous brothers who worked on the design of all-wing aircraft), Oblt. Hubertus von Holtey, Major Ernst von Berg (the Kommandeur), Lt. Hans-Joachim Müncheberg (Gruppenadjutant), Hptm. der Res. Wilde and Hptm. der Res. Michel.

September–December 1939

Stab I./JG 51
Personal emblem of Lt. Ernst Terry

ABOVE AND LEFT: This Bf 109 E marked with a chevron and horizontal bar was flown by Lt. Ernst Terry of the Stab I./JG 51 based at Mannheim-Sandhofen in November 1939. The 'terrier dog' badge was the pilot's personal emblem. Terry claimed two victories in Spain and was later shot down and captured on 29 October 1940 after claiming eight enemy aircraft destroyed.

BELOW: Looking brand new, a pair of Bf 109 Es of I./JG 51 photographed at Mannheim-Sandhofen airfield shortly after the unit was transferred there on 27 October 1939. Note that the aircraft in the background has the Hakenkreuz (Swastika) painted on the fin only and the aircraft in front has yellow gun troughs.

LEFT: This line-up of Bf 109 Es from 5./JG 52, 'Red 5, 6 and 8 can be identified at Böblingen airfield. These aircraft appear to be brand new and were painted RLM 70 and 71 splinter pattern on the uppersurfaces with RLM 65 underneath. They also carried different style red numbers outlined in white to those in the above photo. They also have the new style Balkenkreuz and Hakenkreuz, in the new position applied just on the fin. 'Red 5' in the foreground also had yellow (RLM 04) gun trays.

RIGHT: A Party official, possibly the Gauleiter of Mannheim, examines the cockpit of one of I./JG 51's Bf 109s during a visit to Sandhofen airfield shortly after the Gruppe was transferred there on 27 October 1939. The Gruppe's emblem – a mountain goat looking backwards – referred to the Bavarian town of Bad Aibling where it was formed. The emblem first appeared in the early autumn of 1939.

I./JG 51 badge

LEFT: Taken shortly after II./JG 52 arrived at Mannheim-Sandhofen airfield at the beginning of November 1939, this photo shows the almost factory finish applied to its Bf 109 Es. Mannheim was the second airfield used by II./JG 52, the unit moving from Böblingen at the end of October. In the photo are 'Red 2, 4 and 9' with the thicker than normal white outline making the numbers appear fatter than usual.

September–December 1939

LEFT: Hptm. Hubert Kroeck, Staffelkapitän of 4./JG 53 talks to his pilots at Mannheim-Sandhofen in November 1939. His aircraft, coded 'White 1', also carried the top hat badge plus the famous 'Pik–As' (Ace of spades) emblem of JG 53.

Hptm. Hubert Kroeck's 'top hat' badge as carried on his Bf 109 E

RIGHT: Hptm. Hubert Kroeck (left) congratulates Hptm. Douglas Pitcairn sometime after his first victory on 25 September 1939. Kroeck had previously flown with 2.J/88 and Pitcairn with 3.J/88 in Spain, the former re-using the 'Zylinderhut' (top hat) on his aircraft after transferring to JG 53. Pitcairn was a direct descendant of a Scottish family from Perthshire.

LEFT: After the end of the war in Spain, several pilots who had served in that country with the Condor Legion brought the 'Zylinderhut' insignia with them to their Luftwaffe units. This photo shows a version of the emblem which Hptm. Hubert Kroeck, Staffelkapitän of 4./JG 53 brought to that Geschwader.

JG 53 'Pik As' badge

LEFT: Uffz. Eduard Koslowski of 9./JG 53 pictured in front of his Bf 109 E coded 'Yellow 10' sometime in October/November 1939.

September–December 1939

LEFT: Mechanics unload oil drums from a cart being drawn by cows at Kirchberg, in south-west Germany in November 1939. The Bf 109 E in the background was piloted by Oblt. Wilfried Balfanz of Stab I./JG 53. It has a black chevron and two vertical bars, ostensibly allocated to a 'Major beim Stab'. In practice most of these staff symbols could be carried by pilots with a different position to that indicated.

BELOW: Mechanics of I./JG 53 assist the Gruppe's Technical Officer, Hptm. Dr. Erich Mix from his Bf 109 E marked with a chevron and circle. At this time, late November 1939, I./JG 53 experimented with various types of camouflage patterns.

BELOW: This Bf 109 E was piloted by Hptm. Dr Erich Mix, Gruppe Technische Offizier of I./JG 53. It carries the black single chevron and circle allocated to a Technical Officer with the 'Pik-As' badge of JG 53 on the nose. Photographed at Darmstadt-Griesheim at the end of November 1939, the aircraft has two 'kills' painted on the rudder.

Messerschmitt Bf 109 E-3 Hptm. Dr. Erich Mix, Stab I./JG 53, Wiesbaden-Erbenheim, November 1939
At this time, JG 53 was experimenting with various camouflage colours and patterns. Mix's aircraft carried a splinter pattern of dark green (RLM 71), RLM grey (RLM 02) and pale grey (possibly RLM 63) on the uppersurfaces with pale blue (RLM 65) underneath. The single chevron and circle marking was usually allocated to a Technical Officer.

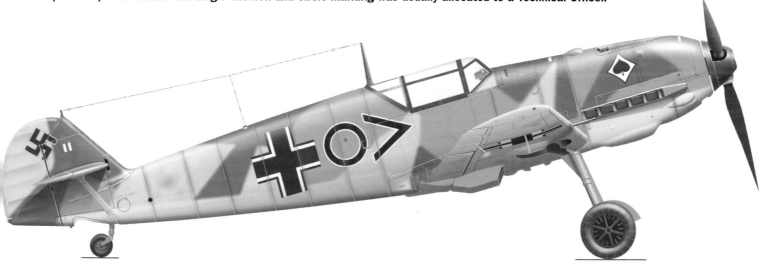

September–December 1939

RIGHT: On 6 November 1939, Uffz. Eduard Koslowski of 9./JG 53 was forced to belly land his Bf 109 E, 'Yellow 10' after shooting down a Mureaux 117 N° 66 of GAO I/506, his first victory. Note again the large splinter pattern segments as applied to the Bf 109 Es of JG 53 at this time.

LEFT AND BELOW: This Fieseler Kassel-built Bf 109 E-3, 'White 1' W.Nr. 1304 of 1./JG 76 landed by mistake at Strasbourg–Woerth airfield in France, only 10 km from the German border, on 22 November 1939, the pilot Fw. Karl Hier being captured. The aircraft was subsequently tested by the CEMA (centre d'essai de matériel aérien, later renamed CEV) at Orléans-Bricy, It was transferred to the test centre at Farnborough, England in January 1940 where it was damaged during a test flight. It was repaired and sent to the USAAF test centre at Wright Field in Dayton, Ohio where it was eventually destroyed on 3 November 1942. Fw. Karl Hier was released from captivity in June 1940 and was able to re-join his Staffel. However he was killed in action on 15 November 1940 near London, in aerial combat with Spitfires .

Badge of JG 76 (later II./JG 54)

Messerschmitt Bf 109 E-3 W.Nr. 1304 of 1./JG 76 captured by French forces at Woerth, Bas-Rhin on 22 November 1939
This aircraft landed intact by mistake in France due to thick fog. The badge represents the arms of the town of Aspern, near Wien, where 1./JG 76 (formerly 1./JG 138) was formed. The uppersurfaces were painted black-green (RLM 70) with light blue (RLM 65) underneath.

September–December 1939

LEFT: Bf 109 E-1 'Red 9', W.Nr. 3326 of 2./JG 51 was flown by Uffz. Georg Pavenzinger on 28 September 1939. After taking off from Speyer the pilot had become disorientated due to strong winds at high altitude and made an emergency landing at Geutertheim due to shortage of fuel and was the first complete Bf 109 E-1 to fall into allied hands. The pilot was taken prisoner and the aircraft moved under a tree to camouflage it from the air. German fighters made several strafing attacks in order to destroy the aircraft but inflicted only minor damage. Eventually the aircraft was transported to Nancy and repaired for flight testing but was damaged on its first test flight. It was repaired again and flown to England for further evaluation.

RIGHT: Piloted by Lt. Heinz Schultz, this Bf 109 E, W.Nr. 1251, 'Yellow 11' of 3./JG 76 was shot down near Sarguemines in December 1939. The pilot survived and was made a prisoner of war. The aircraft was finished in black–green (RLM 70) upper surfaces with light-blue (RLM 65) underneath. It also had the badge of I./JG 76 (later adopted by II./JG 54) just in front of the cockpit.

LEFT: A French officer inspects the cockpit of W. Nr. 1231 with a French soldier carrying his Lebel rifle standing guard. This machine was later transported to Paris and was shown at an exhibition at the Avenue des Champs-Elysées department store where it caused considerable interest.

RIGHT: Under the eyes of fascinated Parisiens the disassembled Bf 109 is unloaded off a truck for transportation into the department store where it was used to raise funds for the French war effort. It is interesting to note that the original Hakenkreuz has been removed and replaced by a very crudely painted replacement on the rudder.

September–December 1939

BELOW: This badge depicting a knight slaying a dragon was possibly carried by a Bf 109 E of JGr 101 during October/November 1939.

Detail of dragon badge of Stab JGr 101 a temporary designation of II./ZG 1

ABOVE LEFT AND ABOVE: This dragon badge was carried by some Bf 109 Es of the Stab of JGr 101. The badge was quite small and was positioned just behind the brown oil filler triangle. The legend 'Start 5.11.39' on the photo above, may refer to the cold starting instructions for the aircraft.

Badge possibly of 2./JGr 101 or later 4./ZG 1

RIGHT: A line up of Bf 109 Es from 5./ZG 1 probably photographed at Fürstenwalde airfield in August 1939 shortly before the invasion of Poland. The aircraft carried the unit's red running dog badge on their engine cowlings together with red numbers outlined in white.

ABOVE AND ABOVE LEFT: The running dog badge of 2./JGr 101 was carried on the nose of Bf 109 Es (probably at Schleswig) in autumn 1939. The unit was originally formed at Bad Aibling on 1 July 1938 as II./JG 135 under Major Stoltenhoff. For a very short time it received the temporary designation I./JG 54 before becoming I./JG 333 under Major Reichardt on 4 November 1938. On 12 May 1939 it was transferred to Fürstenwalde and equipped with the Bf 109 E-1, then being renamed II./ZG 1. Between 21 September 1939 and 1 March 1940, the temporary designation JGr 101 was applied before it was equipped with the Bf 110.

LEFT: One of 2./JGr 101's mechanics, technician Philipp Schmelzer, pictured in front of a Bf 109 E, probably at Schleswig in northern Germany in November 1939. The unit's running dog emblem was quite spectacular.

2./JGr 101 (later 5./ZG 1) running dog badge

Messerschmitt Bf 109 E-1 of 2./JGr 101, Fürstenwalde, August 1939
This unit was temporarily renamed on 21 September 1939, resuming its original designation on 1 March 1940 when it was re-equipped with the Bf 110. The aircraft was painted in a splinter pattern of black-green (RLM 70) and dark green (RLM 71) on the uppersurfaces with light blue (RLM 65) underneath. The 'running dog' badge was a feature of the unit's aircraft at this time.

Jagdwaffe Order of Battle
15 December 1939

(Units in Bold were formed after 1 September 1939)

Stab JG 1	Bf 109 E	Jever	*Obstlt.* Carl Schumacher
II./JG 77	Bf 109 E	Jever, Wangerooge	*Major* Harry von Bülow
II.(J)/186	Bf 109 E	Nordholz	*Hptm.* Heinrich Seeliger
JGr 101[1]	Bf 109 E	Neumünster	*Major* Reichardt
10.(N)/JG 26	**Bf 109 E**	**Jever**	***Oblt.* Johannes Steinhoff**
Stab JG 2	Bf 109 E	Frankfurt-Rebstock	*Oberst* Gerd von Massow
I./JG 2	Bf 109 E	Frankfurt-Rebstock	*Hptm.* Jürgen Roth
II./JG 2	Bf 109 E	Zerbst	*Major* Wolfgang Schellmann
Stab JG 26	Bf 109 E	Dortmund	*Major* Hans-Hugo Witt
I./JG 26	Bf 109 E	Dortmund	*Major* Gotthard Handrick
II./JG 26	Bf 109 E	Werl	*Hptm.* Herwig Knüppel
III./JG 26	**Bf 109 E**	**Essen-Mülheim**	***Major* Ernst von Berg**
***Stab* JG 27**	**Bf 109 E**	**Münster-Handorf**	***Obstlt.* Max Ibel**
I./JG 27	**Bf 109 E**	**Plantlünne, Krefeld**	***Hptm.* Helmut Riegel**
I./JG 1	Bf 109 E	Vörden	*Hptm.* Bernhard Woldenga
***Stab* JG 51**	**Bf 109 E**	**Münster, Bönninghardt**	***Oberst* Theodor Osterkamp**
I./JG 51	Bf 109 E	Krefeld	*Hptm.* Hans-Heinrich Brustellin
I./JG 20	Bf 109 E	Döberitz, Bönninghardt	*Hptm.* Hannes Trautloft
***Stab* JG 52**	**Bf 109 E**	**Mannheim-Sandhofen**	***Major* Hubertus Merhardt von Bernegg**
I./JG 52	Bf 109 E	Lachen-Speyerdorf	*Hptm.* Siegfried von Eschwege
II./JG 52	**Bf 109 E**	**Mannheim-Sandhofen**	***Hptm.* Hans-Günter von Kornatzki**
Stab JG 53	Bf 109 E	Wiesbaden	*Oberst* Hans Klein
I./JG 53	Bf 109 E	Wiesbaden, Darmstadt	*Hptm.* Lothar von Janson
II./JG 53	Bf 109 E	Mannheim-Sandhofen	*Hptm.* Günther von Maltzahn
III./JG 53	**Bf 109 E**	**Wiesbaden**	***Hptm.* Werner Mölders**
***Stab* JG 77**	**Bf 109 E**	**Bonn-Hangelar**	***Obstlt.* Eitel-Fritz Roediger von Manteuffel**
I./JG 77	Bf 109 E	Köln, Oldendorf	*Hptm.* Johannes Janke
II./JG 51	**Bf 109 E**	**Eutingen**	***Hptm.* Ernst Günther Burggaller**
I./JG 54	**Bf 109 E**	**Böblingen**	***Major* Hans-Jürgen von Cramon Taubadel or *Hptm.* Hubertus von Bonin**
I./JG 76	Bf 109 E	Frankfurt-Main	*Hptm.* Winfried von Müller-Rienzburg
I./JG 21	Bf 109 D	Münster, Hopsten	*Hptm.* Martin Mettig
I.(J)/LG 2	Bf 109 E	Köln-Gymnich	*Major* Hanns Trübenbach
I./JG 3	Bf 109 E	Berlin area	*Hptm.* Günther Lützow

1   *JGr 101 was a temporary designation of II.Gruppe ZG 1.*

Spinner identity colours of I./JG1
(colour band widths could vary from one aircraft to another)

Gruppenstab   **1.Staffel**

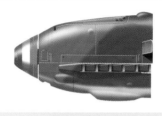

2.Staffel   **3.Staffel**

Schematic position of upper wing Balkenkreuze on the Bf 109

Up until end of September 1939

From October 1939

From beginning of 1940

September–December 1939

Badge of Stab JG 1

RIGHT: Oberstleutnant Carl Schumacher, in his Bf 109 E carrying the badge of JG 1 which shows an eagle defending the German Bight. This area was recognised as being a real Achilles Heel for Germany.

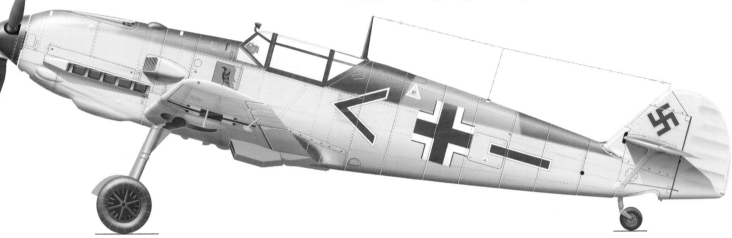

Messerschmitt Bf 109 E-1 flown by Obstlt. Carl Schumacher, Kommodore of JG 1, December 1939

This unit operated against RAF Wellingtons attempting to bomb German naval ships in the German Bight. The uppersurfaces were painted in a splinter pattern of RLM grey (RLM 02) and dark green (RLM 71) with light blue (RLM 65) on the fuselage sides and underneath.

BELOW: Major Carl Schumacher Kommandeur of II./JG 77, was promoted to Oberstleutnant on 12 November 1939 and appointed Kommodore of the newly created Stab JG 1. His new command included the control of II./JG 77, II.(J)/186, JGr 101 and 10.(N)/JG 26. It was this re-organised force that was responsible for the severe losses sustained by the RAF during December 1939.

ABOVE: Only the Stabsschwarm of JG 1 had this emblem on their Bf 109 Es from 1 November 1939 until the end of 1940. The Geschwader was made up of various Gruppen from other units (see Jagdwaffe Order of Battle for 15 December 1939 on page 276) with the command stationed in the Wilhelmshaven-Bremerhaven area. The main task of the unit was to protect the German Bight from enemy activity.

September–December 1939

LEFT: Pilots of 3./JG 51 pictured with one of their Bf 109 Es at Mannheim-Sandhofen in November 1939, shortly after the Gruppe had transferred to this airfield. In the centre of the photo (holding the terrier) is the Staffelkapitän, Hptm. Erich Gerlitz with his Staffeloffizier, Lt. Richard Leppla, to his left. The aircraft carries the 'Totenhand' (the Hand of Death) emblem of 3./JG 51 in a different position to the aircraft shown below.

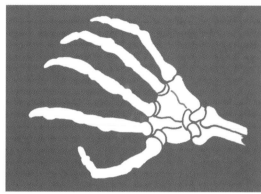

'Totenhand' badge of 3./JG 51

RIGHT: Bf 109 E of 3./JG 51, 'Yellow 3'. This aircraft carries a variety of non standard markings; firstly, the abnormal size of the upper wing crosses. Also the fuselage Balkenkreuz appears to have a slightly narrower black centre but with the new style wider white angle. The Hakenkreuz is still of the old style across the fin and rudder.

I./JG 51 badge

Messerschmitt Bf 109 E-3 of 3./JG 51, winter 1939-1940
This aircraft of this unit, which was based at Mannheim and Krefeld, had overall black–green (RLM 70) uppersurfaces with light blue (RLM 65) underneath. I./JG 51 was formed as I./JG 135 at Bad Aibling, receiving the interim designation I./JG 233. The unit carried variations from previous designations of the 'Kitzbüheler Gams' (Kitzbühel Goat) badge in memory that the Gruppe was expanded by an influx of Austrian pilots in 1938. 3./JG 51 (previously 3./JG 233) also carried the 'Totenhand' (the hand of death) on its aircraft. Note also the yellow (RLM 04) gun troughs.

September–December 1939

RIGHT: Another successful pilot during the operation against RAF bombers on 18 December 1939 was Fw. Hans Troitzsch of 6./JG 77 who shot down two Wellingtons. Here a mechanic looks at the three victory painted bars on the tail of Troitzsch's Bf 109 E. He made his first claim against a Wellington on 4 September 1939.

Messerschmitt Bf 109 E-1 of 6.(J)/Trägergruppe 186, winter 1939/1940

This aircraft carried the splinter camouflage pattern of black-green (RLM 70) and dark green (RLM 71) with light blue (RLM 65) underneath. II.(J)/186, was later redesignated III./JG 77 and joined Oberstleutnant Carl Schumacher's JG 1 which operated against RAF bombers attacking the German fleet in the German Bight. The 6.(J)/186 carried a distinctive emblem showing a witch on a broomstick.

Badge of 6.(J)/186
(later redesignated III./JG 77).

ABOVE: A Bf 109 E of 6.(J)/186, 'Yellow 14', with the 'witch on a broomstick' emblem.

ABOVE AND RIGHT: The witch riding a broomstick badge was successively carried by the Bf 109 Es of 6.(J)186. Due to the complicated nature of the emblem it can be seen, from these three photos, that the colours of the badge varied much from one machine to another. It is probable that although similar every aircraft carried a completely unique badge in different colours.

Only a few bursts were necessary to send the bomber falling into sea...

GEORG SCHIRMBÖCK

O n 18 December 1939, I took off with the rest of 5./JG 77 to intercept a formation of RAF Wellington bombers making for the German Bight. We soon found the Wellingtons and I immediately opened fire on one which was flying behind and to the left of the remaining bombers. The rear gunner of the bomber flying at the head of the group then returned fire. I had a trouble with my machine-guns and had to finish 'my' bomber with cannon fire. I was slightly wounded but managed to reach Wangerooge to make an emergency landing.

ABOVE: Lt. Georg Schirmböck of 6./JG 77 climbs from the cockpit of his Bf 109 E following the action in which he shot down an RAF Wellington on 18 December 1939. This operation was later re-enacted for the benefit of PK (Propaganda Company) cameramen.

ABOVE: A mechanic from 6./JG 77 painting a first victory bar on the fin of Lt. Georg Schirmböck's Bf 109 E. This was scored on 18 December 1939 when the RAF lost fifteen Wellingtons to the German fighter force in the German Bight area.

II./JG 77 badge as depicted on Lt. Winfried Schmidt's Bf 109 E and his personal 'top hat' emblem

...my claim...it would certainly never be confirmed.

WINFRIED SCHMIDT

With Lt. Georg Schirmböck, Lt. Winfried Schmidt is one of the few survivors of this action. He also remembers his first claim.

D uring the summer of 1939, I was recalled to the *Luftwaffe* and posted to *Oblt.* Alfred von Lojewski's 5./JG 77 based in the German Bight area. It was here that I took part in the first major combat between the *Jagdwaffe* and the RAF on 18 December 1939. By the time I arrived, the action was almost over. I thought I had no chance of gaining a good position to attack when I saw a single

Lt. Winfried Schmidt gives the thumbs-up after his successful mission.

bomber trying to escape. I dived in his direction and managed to position my Bf 109 '*Kölle alaaf*' in a good shooting position behind him. Only a few bursts were necessary to send the bomber falling into the sea. I was lucky, but more than I had supposed at that moment. When I returned to base, I filed my claim but my *Staffelkapitän* told me that it would certainly never be confirmed. I had to provide two witnesses, one in the air and the other on the ground but the fighting took place in the air! Fortunately, one of my *Staffel* comrades saw my victory and confirmed it, and we were not long receiving a telegram from the Navy. A seaman on board a destroyer had described my action and given the number of my plane. Both reports were sent to OKL *(Oberkommando der Luftwaffe)*, and I thus received official confirmation of my claim.

September–December 1939

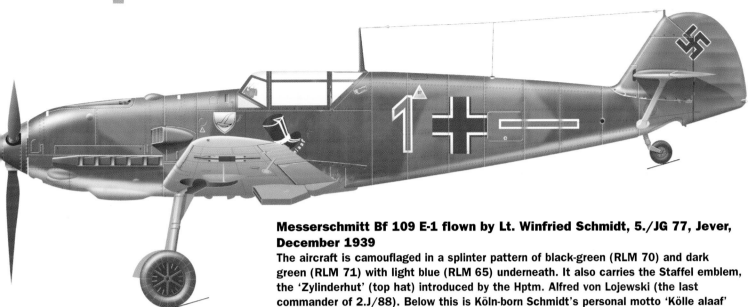

Messerschmitt Bf 109 E-1 flown by Lt. Winfried Schmidt, 5./JG 77, Jever, December 1939
The aircraft is camouflaged in a splinter pattern of black-green (RLM 70) and dark green (RLM 71) with light blue (RLM 65) underneath. It also carries the Staffel emblem, the 'Zylinderhut' (top hat) introduced by the Hptm. Alfred von Lojewski (the last commander of 2.J/88). Below this is Köln-born Schmidt's personal motto 'Kölle alaaf' (literally 'Up Köln' – the title of one of the songs used in the city's carnival procession). Forward of these two emblems is the first insignia used by II./JG 77, a seagull.

II./JG 77
'Seagull' emblem as shown below,
(note variation to the badge on
Lt. Winfried Schmidt's Bf 109 E)

ABOVE: Pictured a few hours after claiming his first victory on 18 December 1939, a RAF Wellington, Lt. Winfried Schmidt of 5./JG 77 poses in front of his Bf 109 E-1 coded 'Red 1' at Jever in the German Bight area. Note the Staffel emblem, the Zylinderhut (top hat) reintroduced by the Staffelkapitän, Hptm. Alfred von Lojewski (a former pilot with 2.J/88). Below this is Schmidt's personal motto 'Kölle alaaf' (literally 'Up Cologne' – used in the city's carnival procession), the pilot having been born in that city. Forward of these two emblems is the seagull emblem of II./JG 77.

ABOVE: Oblt. Anton Pointner of 5./JG 77 seated in the cockpit of his Bf 109 in the German Bight area, November 1939. At this time, the Gruppe's badge comprised a seagull in flight. Later this was replaced by an eagle's head in flight over the water.

LEFT Mechanics overhauling a Bf 109 E of II./JG 77 probably at Jever during November 1939. The unit was to have many successes against RAF aircraft attempting to bomb the German fleet around Wilhelmshaven.

September–December 1939

All I was interested in was learning to fly.

JULIUS MEIMBERG

I was born on 11 January 1917 at Münster. I began flying gliders in 1935, progressively switching to powered aircraft. After completing our examinations, sixteen of our group of twenty-four became officer pilots. The training was difficult, especially the technical studies. At this stage I did not known whether I would become a fighter, bomber or *Stuka* pilot. All I was interested in was learning to fly. My flying instruction was soon interrupted by course work, six months, all very hard! Then I was posted to the *Luftkriegsschule* at Berlin-Gatow where I received military training, essentially drill (which I didn't like much), formation flying (much more pleasant) and tactical awareness for officers (more theory). During this period, we made several tours (each between three and four weeks long) to different units such as I./JG 53 at Wiesbaden. This all took about two years, from 1937 to 1939. At the beginning of the war, I was a *Leutnant*. One of my comrades promoted at the same time as me was Bernd Gallowitsch who was later awarded the *Ritterkreuz*.

In October 1939 I was sent to the *Jagdfliegerschule* at Schleissheim where I met, among others, two subsequently famous pilots, Egon Mayer and Gerhard Barkhorn. I remained at this school for about a month before receiving my final posting to II./JG 2 at Zerbst. I was sent to the fourth *Staffel* under *Oblt.* Hans 'Assi' Hahn which was just being formed.

Thus I came to JG 2 by chance. This unit, which carried on the famous 'Richthofen' name and tradition was not an élite *Geschwader* as has often been said. However, because it was the first *Geschwader* in the new *Luftwaffe*, many of the best and more experienced pilots often stayed with it rather than go to newly created units. This might have been the reason for the excellence of its pilots. Another reason which someone told me but I'm not sure if it is correct, was that our *Gruppenkommandeur* was Wolfgang Schellmann who created II./JG 2. I was told that after his service in Spain and Poland, he was posted to an administrative position where his main occupation was personnel. Because of that he was able to select the best people for II./JG 2 when he began its formation.

A few weeks after my arrival at 4./JG 2, our Gruppe left the Berlin area and moved to Nordholz, a former Zeppelin field between Hamburg and Cuxhaven. It was very quiet around that area with no opportunities for combat. Just before the *'Westfeldzug'* (the campaign against France, Belgium and the Low Countries) my *Staffel* moved to my home town of Münster in western Germany.

When 4./JG 2 was formed at Zerbst in the middle of December 1939, one of its younger pilots was Lt. Julius Meimberg. The 22 year-old officer was awarded the Ritterkreuz five years later as commander of II./JG 53. The aircraft in the to the left of the picture is a He 70.

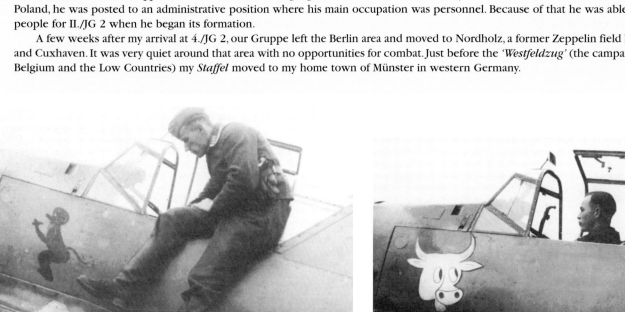

ABOVE: The personal emblem of the 'laughing cow' was carried on the Bf 109 E 'White 4' of Fw. Erwin Weiss of 4./JG 53

BOTTOM OPPOSITE AND THIS PAGE: In the autumn of 1939 pilots of 4./JG 53 painted personal emblems on the fuselage sides of their Bf 109 Es. Unfortunately the identity of most of the pilots is unknown. These Bf 109 Es of 4./JG 53 were painted in a splinter pattern similar to that shown on page 253, of irregular patches of light–blue (RLM 65), RLM grey (RLM 02) and dark green (RLM 71).

September–December 1939

**Personal badge of
Hptm. Hennig Strümpell
while with 3./JG 2**

ABOVE, RIGHT AND RIGHT CENTRE: These three photos plus the other two on this page were taken by the German PK (Propaganda Kompanie) to publicise the first victories claimed by JG 2 on 22 November 1939 by Lt. Helmut Wick and Ofw. Erwin Kley (both with 3./JG 2). He adopted he top hat insignia as a personal emblem. This Bf 109 E, W.Nr. 921 piloted by the Staffelkapitän, Hptm. Hennig Strümpell was based at Frankfurt-Rebstock. The pilot in the right centre photo is Erwin Kley pointing to his two victories painted on the fin of his Bf 109 E, although only one was officially confirmed.

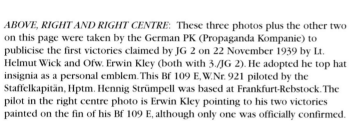

Badge of 3./JG 2 'Richthofen'

ABOVE: When Hptm. Hennig Strümpell, who was born in Pomerania, took over command of 3./JG 2, he brought with him the triangular blue flag of that region. The flag was painted in blue on the engine cowling of some of the unit's Bf 109 Es together with the motto 'Horrido!' (best translated as 'Tally-ho!'). Lt. Helmut Wick was later to use this flag as a personal emblem. Note the large national insignia crosses painted on the wing uppersurfaces and the partly obliterated number '1' which is probably where the censor had not done the job properly of removing it before allowing the photo to be published.

RIGHT: Hptm. Hennig Strümpell, Staffelkapitän of 3./JG 2 taxies through the winter snow of 1939-1940 at Frankfurt-Rebstock airfield in his Bf 109 E.

September–December 1939

ABOVE: Oberst Gerd von Massow, seated in his Bf 109 E. He was Kommodore of JG 2 from autumn 1936 until March 1940.

ABOVE: The Bf 109 E-1 flown by Oberst von Massow who before he became Kommodore of JG 2 commanded JFS 2 (Jagdfliegerschule 2) in Schleissheim. The upper part of the fuselage was painted in RLM Grey (RLM 02) and dark green (RLM 71) with the sides and underneath in light blue (RLM 65).

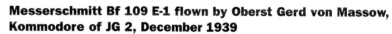

Messerschmitt Bf 109 E-1 flown by Oberst Gerd von Massow, Kommodore of JG 2, December 1939
It is interesting to compare this aircraft with von Massow's Bf 109 D-1 illustrated in Jagdwaffe Section 1 (Birth of the Luftwaffe) page 82. The two horizontal bars were retained but with the addition of a chevron and the number '1' in black outlined in white - the latter indicating the first aircraft in the Stabsschwarm.

JG 2 'Richthofen Geschwader' badge

RIGHT: This Bf 109 E from JG 2 has an interesting combination of national markings. The oversize upper wing crosses introduced in October 1939 and the new style wide white angled Balkenkreuz on the fuselage. However it still retains the old position of the Hakenkreuz over the fin and rudder.

September–December 1939

Messerschmitt Bf 109 E-1 flown by Oblt. Franz Hörnung, Staffelkapitän of 1./JG 26, Dortmund, December 1939
Around this time, the Luftwaffe began to paint the fuselage sides of their Bf 109s pale blue (RLM 65) as standard with a splinter pattern of RLM grey (RLM 02) and dark green (RLM 71) on the uppersurfaces together with a modified Balkenkreuz with increased white area. This also aircraft carries the grasshopper emblem of the first Staffel.

1./JG 26 badge

BELOW: A Kette from 1./JG 26 'Grasshopper' Staffel revving up for take off in the snow during the winter of 1939-1940

ABOVE: Close-up of the 1./JG 26 'Grasshopper' badge, although the Bf 109 E has black-green (RLM 70) coloured fuselage sides.

ABOVE: A brand new Bf 109 E-1 is pushed out into the snow from the assembly hall. The aircraft still carries its radio call sign and is painted light blue (RLM 65) all over except for the spinner and propeller which have the standard finish of black green (RLM 70).

ABOVE: A pilot and two 'black men' from 1./JG 51 pose behind a battery charger, with a Bf 109 E, coded 'White 5' in the background. This photo was taken at Mannheim-Sandhofen or Krefeld airfield during December 1939. 'Black men' was a nickname given to Luftwaffe mechanics because of the colour of the overalls they wore.

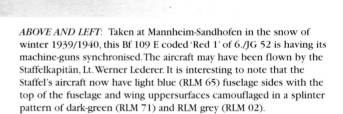

ABOVE AND LEFT: Taken at Mannheim-Sandhofen in the snow of winter 1939/1940, this Bf 109 E coded 'Red 1' of 6./JG 52 is having its machine-guns synchronised. The aircraft may have been flown by the Staffelkapitän, Lt. Werner Lederer. It is interesting to note that the Staffel's aircraft now have light blue (RLM 65) fuselage sides with the top of the fuselage and wing uppersurfaces camouflaged in a splinter pattern of dark-green (RLM 71) and RLM grey (RLM 02).

BELOW: Luftwaffe 'black men' check the radio equipment on a Bf 109 E, coded 'Red 13' of 2./JG 52 probably at Mannheim-Sandhofen during December 1939. Note the 'Rabatz' (trouble-maker) Staffel emblem painted on the nose, a naked baby devil with a bow and arrow. This Staffel's aircraft were painted in a splinter pattern of black green (RLM 70) and dark-green (RLM 71) on the uppersurfaces with light blue (RLM 65) on the sides of the fuselage and underneath.

2./JG 52 badge

September–December 1939

RIGHT: Pilots from II./JG 77 photographed on 18 December 1939 after combat with RAF bombers. With his back to camera is the Kommandeur Harry von Bülow. First from the left is Lt. Alfred von Lojewski (former leader of 2.J/88), Staffelkapitän of 5./JG 77 from July 39 to June 40. He claimed one aircraft destroyed 14 December.

Badge of II./JG 77 from early 1940

ABOVE AND RIGHT: At the end of December 1939, II./JG 77 transferred to the windswept North Sea island of Wangerooge. The aircraft in the foreground is the Bf 109 E belonging to the Kommandeur of the Gruppe, Harry von Bülow. Despite experiencing several warm days in late December 1939 and early January 1940, the unit saw little action. Note the rush matting over the centre of the fuselage to obscure the markings.